FROMELLES

First published in 2011 by black dog books

This edition reprinted in 2012
by black dog books,
an imprint of Walker Books Australia Pty Ltd
Locked Bag 22, Newtown
NSW 2042 Australia
www.walkerbooks.com.au

Maps by Guy Holt Design
Printed and bound in Australia by Griffin Press

National Library of Australia cataloguing-in-publication data:
Wilkinson, Carole, 1950–
Fromelles: Australia's bloodiest day at war / Carole Wilkinson
ISBN: 978 1 742031 76 7 (pbk.)
Series: The Drum.
For secondary school age
Subjects: Fromelles, Battle of, Fromelles, France, 1916.
World War, 1914–1918 – Campaigns – France – Juvenile literature.
World War, 1914–1918 – Participation, Australian – Juvenile literature.
Australian – History, Military – Juvenile literature.
940.4272

10 9 8 7 6 5

black dog books would like to thank Neville Kidd and Damian Madden for their factual checks of this book.

carole WILKINSON

FROMELLES

AUSTRALIA'S BLOODIEST DAY AT WAR

AWM DASEY1446

Private Charles Henry Brear, 60th Battalion, of South Yarra, Victoria, and an unnamed woman. Private Brear was killed in action at Fromelles on 19 July 1916, aged 21.

In war, there are no unwounded soldiers.

— José Narosky

To the memory of my grandfathers and great uncles who took part in World War I
— C.W.

CONTENTS

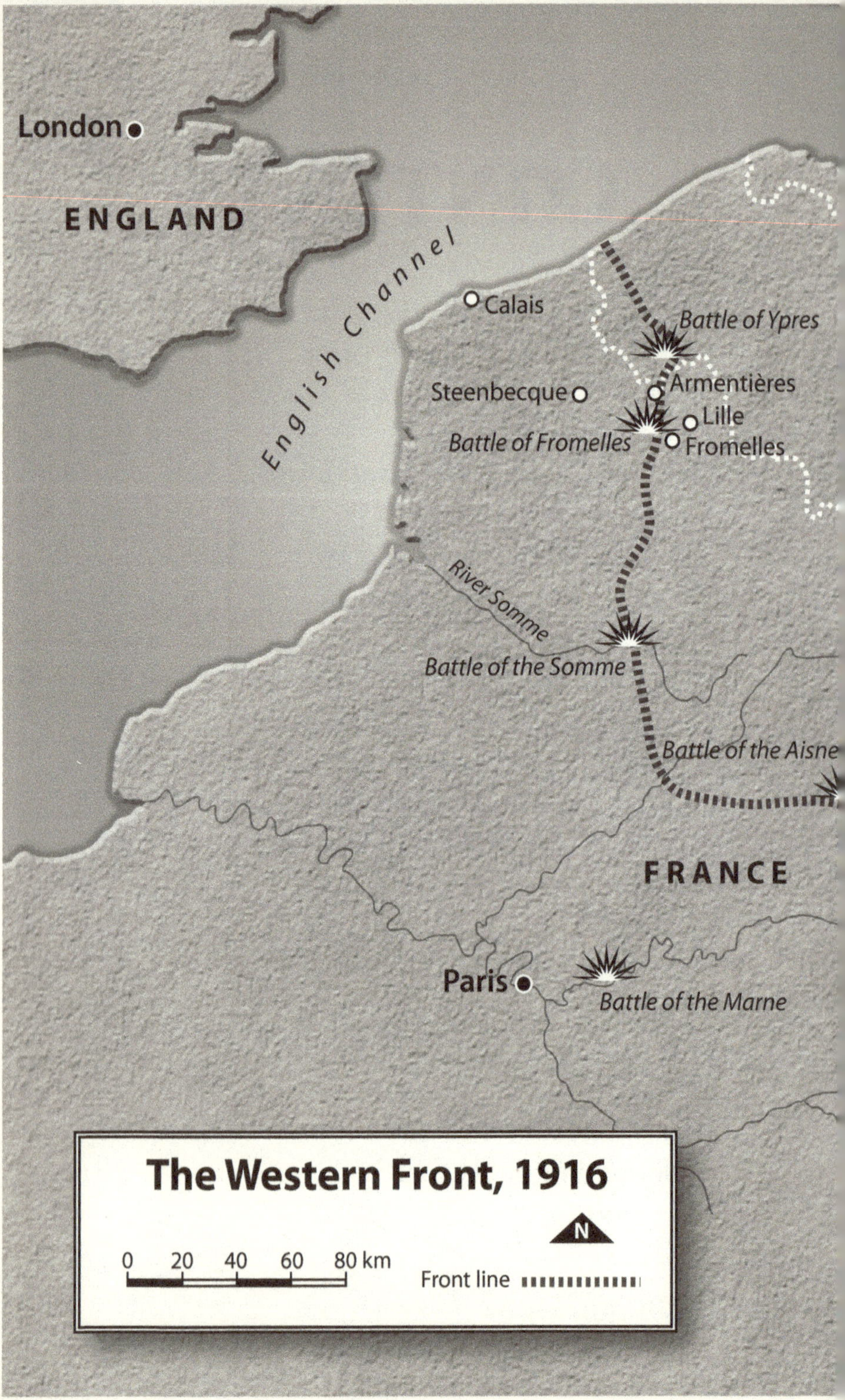
London
ENGLAND
English Channel
Calais
Battle of Ypres
Armentières
Steenbecque
Lille
Battle of Fromelles
Fromelles
River Somme
Battle of the Somme
Battle of the Aisne
FRANCE
Paris
Battle of the Marne
The Western Front, 1916
N
0 20 40 60 80 km
Front line

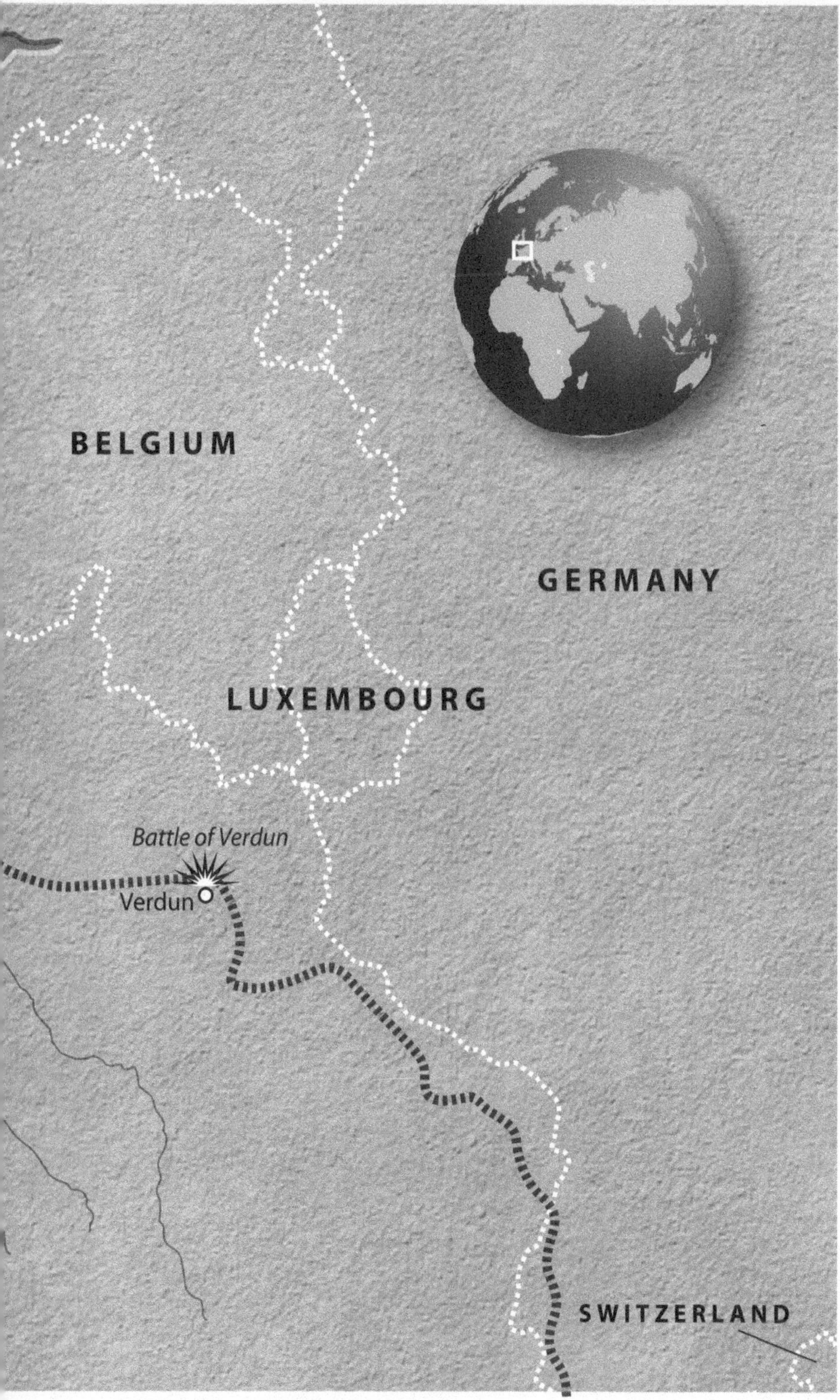
BELGIUM
GERMANY
LUXEMBOURG
Battle of Verdun
Verdun
SWITZERLAND

Introduction

The first shots of the Battle of Fromelles were fired at 11 a.m. on 19 July 1916 in French Flanders near the village of Fromelles. In less than 24 hours, more than 5,000 Australian soldiers were killed, wounded or taken prisoner. More Australian soldiers died in this one battle than in the Boer War, the Korean War and the Vietnam War combined.

The terrible loss of life and suffering was all for nothing. The attack was supposed to trick the Germans into thinking that there was a large force of Allied soldiers in that part of France. British war commanders didn't want more German soldiers to be sent south to the Battle of the Somme, where **the Allies** were failing to break through the German front line. But the Germans were not fooled, and the Allies lost the Battle of Fromelles.

World War I lasted from August 1914 to November 1918. In the history of the world's many wars, it was not a long war. It was called the Great War then, but later, when it needed to be distinguished from the next war, it became known as World War I. The numbers of people involved were certainly great — 65 million combatants. The number of casualties was staggering — 37.5 million. Those who died numbered 8.5 million — that's more than 5,400 people for each day of the war.

Australia was a young country that had only recently united its six separate British colonies under one government. The population of the country was less than 5 million. Keen to prove its nationhood and be worthy of its place in the British Empire, Australia sent its young men to fight in this European war. In total, 416,809 Australian men enlisted, and over 300,000 of them served overseas. More than 60,000 men were killed and 156,000 were injured or taken prisoner — that means almost two-thirds of the Australian soldiers who took part ended up as casualties.

The Battle of Fromelles was just one battle in a terrible war. In the bloody roll call of the dead, wounded and permanently scarred, this small battle stands out as Australia's worst day of this or any other war. It was 24 hours of bravery, bad decisions and pointless loss of life.

World War I Timeline

1 August 1914 — Outbreak of World War I

4 August 1914 — Australia declares war

5–12 September 1914 — First Battle of the Marne

13–28 September 1914 — First Battle of the Aisne

25 April 1915 — Gallipoli landing

19–20 December 1915 — Gallipoli evacuation

14 February 1916 — Fifth Division formed in Egypt

21 February 1916 — Battle of Verdun begins

25 May 1916 — Conscription introduced in Britain

23–30 June 1916 — Fifth Division arrives in France

1 July 1916 — Battle of the Somme begins

8 July 1916 — Fourth Division ordered to go to the Somme

10–11 July 1916 — Fifth Division takes position in front line

12 July 1916 — Fifth Division ordered to take part in a battle at Fromelles

17 July 1916 — Battle postponed

19–20 July 1916 — Battle of Fromelles

17 November 1916 — Battle of the Somme ends

18 December 1916 — Battle of Verdun ends

11 November 1918 — End of World War I

Basic Australian Army Structure

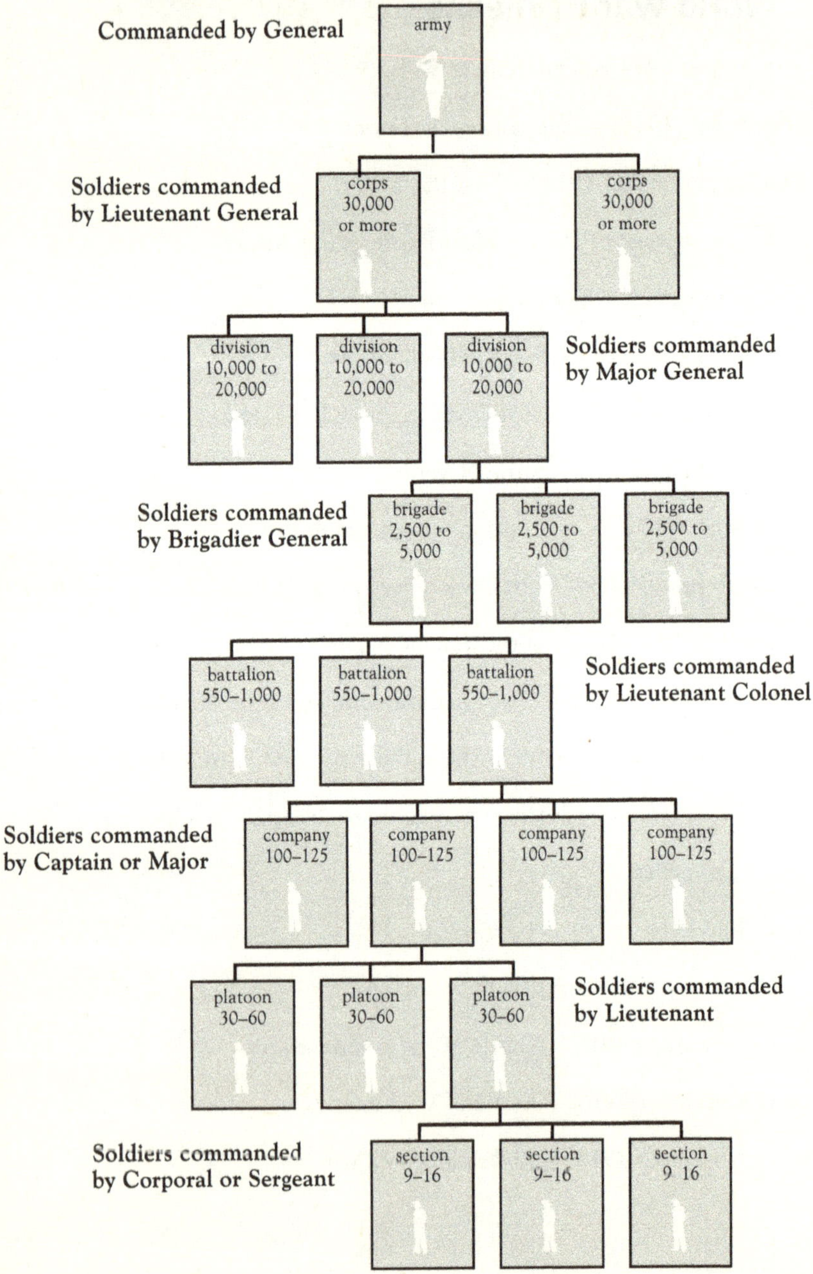

Chapter 1
New Recruits

22 May 1915, Melbourne, Australia
Walter McAlister,
carpenter's apprentice

I'm going to volunteer. I always intended to, the minute I turned 18, but I've had enough, so I'm not waiting any longer. It's not my fault I'm over six foot and I look older than my age, but every day someone, somewhere, has a go at me. Yesterday some boys from the school up the road were chanting, 'Cowardy, cowardy custard, your arms are made of mustard'. It hurts. One of them spat on the footpath in front of me.

Last week I tried to join the Albert Park Football Club, but they wouldn't have me.

'We don't take chickens,' the coach said.

I tried to explain that I'm under-age, but he wouldn't listen.

Mum says I shouldn't take any notice. 'You send 'em round to me,' she says, 'I'll sort 'em out.'

It seems like she's the only person in Melbourne who doesn't want me to join the army.

She's hoping the war will be over before I turn 18 next year.

'You should lie about your age. Tell 'em you're only 16,' she says. 'I want you to stay here with me. Always.'

I gave her a hug. She only comes up to my shoulder. It'll be hard for her when I go, and Billy won't like it either.

As it happens, I've already lied about my age to someone — Sally Tucker. Except I told her that I'm older than I am, not younger.

The first time I walked into the Palais with her on my arm, I felt so proud I thought I'd burst. I wanted to act like it was the most normal thing in the world, but I couldn't wipe the smile off my face.

I shouldn't have told her I was 18 and a half, but she'd just had her 18th birthday when I first asked her out.She wouldn't have said yes if she'd known I was only 17. We've been stepping out together for three months now and I know for sure that Sally's the only girl for me.

We were walking in the Botanical Gardens last Sunday afternoon. She looked a picture in a pink floral dress and a hat that she made herself. Every second bloke was in uniform. They couldn't take their eyes of my Sally. They tipped their hats to her and she smiled at every one of them. She thinks there's nothing smarter than an army uniform.

I left her at a table and went to order two teas and some scones at the kiosk, but the girl behind the counter ignored me, serving everybody else. Then a lady with a poodle and a parasol pushed in front.

'Why aren't you over in Turkey?' she says, prodding me in the stomach with her parasol. 'You should be defending the Empire. If you were a man you would be!'

Her silly-looking dog was barking at me and other people in the queue were nodding and muttering 'traitor'.

I went back to the table where Sally was sitting. Her face was bright red. She picked up her handbag, got up and walked away. I ran after her, pleading with her like a three-year-old. Near the oak lawn, she turned towards me. She didn't speak. She reached up to her hat and pulled out a feather. A white one. She handed it to me, and stupidly, I took it.

I'd heard of women giving white feathers to men who hadn't volunteered, because they thought they were cowards. I never thought it would happen to me. Sally strode off and I stood there on the path with the feather in my hand. It was more grey than white, just a stupid chook feather.

You need your parents' permission to join up if you're under 21. I knew Mum would never agree to it, so I went home and I wrote a letter.

'I am proud that my son, Walter McAlister, has decided to go to war,' I wrote. 'Under the present circumstances,

I reckon it is the duty of every young man to do so. I am willing to let him go.'

I forged Mum's signature, signing it with my left hand.

I'll earn more as a soldier than as a carpenter's apprentice. I can send half my pay home to Mum and still have some savings. I won't waste my money on beer. I'm going to save up for an engagement ring. When I get back Sally'll know I'm not a coward and I'll ask her to marry me.

I'm at the recruitment office. There's a queue of young men, and some not so young, all keen to join up.

The recruitment officer looks at my letter with the wonky signature.

'How old are you, sonny?' he says.

'Eighteen and a half,' I say.

He looks at me. Then he winks and hands me an enlistment form.

WORLD WAR I began with the assassination of the heir to the throne of the Austro-Hungarian Empire. Political tensions in Europe were high, and war was inevitable. When it was revealed that Serbia was responsible for the assassination, Austria declared war on Serbia. Because Russia had an agreement that it would assist Serbia if it were ever attacked, Russia joined the war. The German Empire sided with the Austro-Hungarian Empire, and when the German Army set out to invade France, it first captured the small, neutral country of Belgium. That was the signal for Great Britain to join the war in defence of Belgium and France. Once Britain was involved, then members of the British Empire followed — including Australia.

The war lasted from mid-1914 to the end of 1918.

Enthusiasm

Most of the Australian public were strongly behind the war. They thought it was Australia's duty to fight alongside the 'Mother Country'. At school, children were taught to be proud of Australia's place in the British Empire. Boys and young men between the ages of 12 and 26 took part in compulsory military training — boys in cadets, young men in the home **militia**. Schoolboys had to participate for a number of hours each year in physical education, marching and rifle training. Young men took part in drills and camps.

When war was declared, there were celebrations in the streets. The Australian Prime Minister at the time declared that Australia would defend Britain 'to the last man and last shilling'. Women joined the Red Cross and formed groups of volunteers, called Patriotic Leagues, which sent parcels of food and clothing to soldiers overseas. School children raised money and wrote letters to soldiers. The government sent wool and cloth to schools, for girls to make into clothing for soldiers.

'This Australia of ours, the freest and best country on God's Earth, calls to her sons for aid. History has given you a great opportunity. Now is the hour when you can strike on her behalf.'

Australia's second war-time Prime Minister, William 'Billy' Hughes, December 1915

A Sense of Duty

Australian troops embarked for war service in November 1915. Following training in Egypt, they sailed to Turkey and took part in the Gallipoli Campaign and, after a bitter nine-month struggle, they were evacuated. The evacuation was successful, but the Gallipoli Campaign was not. Even though the campaign had failed, people in Australia didn't turn against the war. The defeat at Gallipoli had made them realise that unless everyone in the

A huge crowd gathers to bid farewell to a contingent of Australian troops bound for war, Melbourne, December 1914.

British Empire committed themselves to the war effort, the unthinkable could happen — they could lose the war.

Conscription in Germany and France had been in place before the war. In 1916, Britain had run out of volunteers willing to die for their country and had just started to conscript new recruits. The Australian government, however, still had enough volunteers — young men who were keen to take part, eager to improve Australia's reputation on this world stage. Although young Australian men were not forced to join the army, the pressure from the civilian population for all able young men to do their duty was very strong. Newspaper articles spoke of Glory and Honour and Duty.

Seeing the casualty lists in papers hadn't reduced the Australian public's enthusiasm for the war. Many believed that men who didn't volunteer were cowards and traitors. Any eligible man who hadn't volunteered might find himself banned from joining clubs, insulted as he walked down the street, refused by any girl he asked out on a date. In the end it was often easier to volunteer.

Many Australian young men were keen to take part in war. They believed they were about to begin the adventure of a lifetime. They were. But not in the way they imagined.

The Gallipoli Inheritance

Australia became a nation in 1901 when the six colonies

united at Federation — just 13 years before war broke out. Soldiers from all of the Australian colonies had fought in the Boer War (1899–1902), but the Gallipoli Campaign was the first time that Australia had been involved in a war as a nation. Australia's soldiers had played a key role at Gallipoli and Australians were proud of the way their soldiers had performed.

'Wherever the Australians and New Zealanders fight in the future, they will take their place in the battle as veterans, as men who have learned to suffer and be strong, to dare to the utmost and be wary, to refuse to admit defeat and to discipline the ardour of inexperience.'

Brisbane Courier, 22 December 1915

Australian soldiers had developed a confidence in their ability to wage war. They had proved that Australian men could hold their own in a battle, just as well, if not better, than the British. The legend of the Anzac spirit had been born.

The defeat at Gallipoli didn't reduce the numbers of Australian volunteers. After Gallipoli, the Prime Minister sent a letter and enlistment form to every man in Australia between the ages of 18 and 44, urging them to volunteer. In January 1916, just a month after the Gallipoli evacuation, more than 22,000 young Australian men volunteered to join the army. They were determined that Australians would be part of a decisive victory in France.

The Western Front

In Europe, the early stages of World War I had involved German and Allied troops fighting in battles across France as they each advanced and retreated. At one stage in 1914, German soldiers advanced so close to Paris that the French government moved to Bordeaux and a million Parisians left the city anticipating that Paris would fall into German hands. But French and British troops succeeded in pushing the Germans back in the Battle of the Marne.

As the German troops retreated in September 1914, they took up positions on high ground on the other side of the Aisne River in northern France. British and French troops tried to take the German position, but failed. The exposed Allies dug trenches to protect themselves from enemy fire. Over the following weeks, as the armies tried to **out-flank** each other, a line of opposing trenches, a kilometre or less apart, lengthened across France.

*When a government forces people to join the army, it is called conscription. A list of all eligible men is compiled and, as soldiers are needed, names are selected at random, for example, by birth date. In the second half of World War I, the Australian government wanted to introduce conscription, but this was defeated in two separate **referenda.***

An Australian World War I recruitment poster by Norman Lindsay.

Eventually, the trenches snaked in a continuous line for 700 kilometres from the coast of Belgium to the border of Switzerland. This line was known as the Western Front. For three years there was a stalemate as both sides fought to gain ground. The position of the Front altered only a few kilometres either way in some areas, until the last few weeks of the war.

When the war began Australian recruits had to be between 18 and 38 years of age, at least 5 feet 6 inches (168 cms) tall and with a chest measurement of at least 34 inches (86 cms). By the end of 1915, the Australian Army was accepting men between 18 and 45, who were 5 feet 2 inches (157 cms) and had a 33 inch chest (84 cms).

The Western Front was divided into sectors and each sector was defended by a **division** of soldiers. The British Army was in charge of most of the northern sectors of the Front. They were supported by divisions from the British Empire's dominions — Australia, New Zealand, Canada and India.

Egyptian Interlude

As they sailed from Australia in 1916, new recruits were keen to start fighting the German Army as soon as possible. But they didn't sail directly to France; they found themselves disembarking in Egypt, where the Australian Training Depot was located.

The new recruits were taken to the Tel-el-Kebir training camp, a tent city that had sprung up in the Egyptian desert. The Australian and New Zealand Army **Corps** (ANZAC), which had served in the war to that point, was expanded and divided into two corps — I ANZAC and II ANZAC. Experienced soldiers who had fought at Gallipoli were mixed with the new recruits to form two new divisions — the Fourth Division and the Fifth Division.

Training in Egypt consisted of fitness drills that were more gruelling versions of those the soldiers had undertaken as cadets.

Scarab beetles were plentiful at Tel-el-Kebir. Bored Australian soldiers would catch one and put it inside a raised circle of sand, make several openings in the circle and then bet on which opening the beetle would use to escape.

Attitude

Australian soldiers were under the command of the British

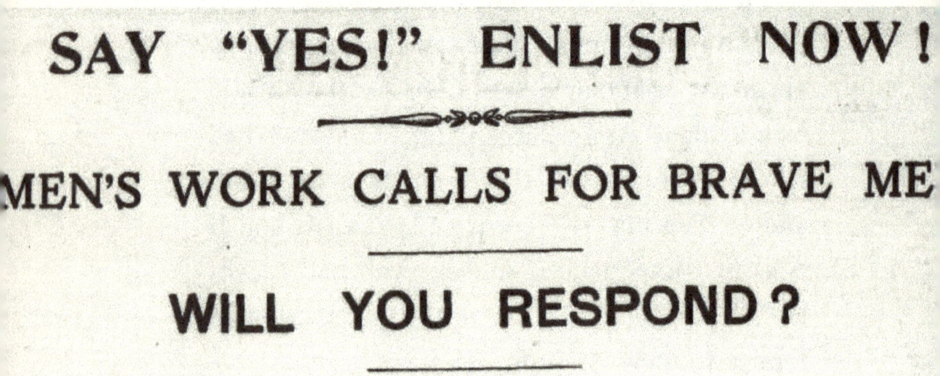
SAY "YES!" ENLIST NOW!

MEN'S WORK CALLS FOR BRAVE ME

WILL YOU RESPOND?

Headline in *The Argus*, Monday 10 January 1916, calling for men to join the Australian Army.

Army, but many Australians didn't appreciate the British style of military discipline. Desert training was boring, and the heat, sand and flies made life very uncomfortable. The Australians weren't interested in discipline and 'spit and polish', and thought officers should only get respect if they'd earned it.

On 25 April 1916, the first anniversary of the landing at Gallipoli, Australian soldiers in Egypt celebrated the very first Anzac Day with a church parade and a sports day that included a football match and an egg and spoon race.

Australian soldiers had a reputation for refusing to salute their officers, and acting insultingly, sometimes violently, towards the Egyptians. They had joined the army to do a job. They couldn't see how constant saluting, endless parade-ground marching and the number of buttons they had done up would have any effect on the way they fought Germans when they went to France.

'Like a colt from a large paddock, [the Australian soldier] at first resented all restraint…even when he had been adequately tamed, over-insistence upon [saluting officers]…seemed to him mere pin-pricking.'

Captain C E W Bean, Official Australian War Historian

The veterans of the Gallipoli Campaign taught the new arrivals Australian disrespect for authority.

'The Australian Training Depot in Egypt has always found the greatest difficulty in producing officers of any value.'

Staff of Sir Archibald Murray, Chief of the Imperial General Staff

The British officers, in turn, had a very low opinion of Australian soldiers and didn't believe that any Australian had the proper characteristics to become an officer.

Desert March

The Fifth Division was one of the newly formed Australian divisions. It was made up of the 15th **Brigade**, which contained Victorians; the 14th Brigade whose soldiers were from New South Wales; and the 8th Brigade that was mainly composed of West Australians, South Australians and Queenslanders. Early in 1916 the command of the Fifth Division was given to Major General James McCay. He had fought at Gallipoli, been wounded there and sent home to recover. Now he had returned to service.

From the beginning, McCay was unpopular with the men serving under him. When the Fifth Division received orders to defend the Suez Canal in Egypt, there was a shortage of transport, so only the 8th Brigade could travel by train. McCay decided to turn the journey to the Suez into a training

'28.3.16. Heat intense. Men collapsing in dozens. Water all done...Hell on earth — an Egyptian desert during the midday heat with an empty water bottle...'

Major Roy Harrison, 54th Battalion, 14th Brigade

The Australian Army held a ballot to decide who would be the official Australian correspondent for World War I. Journalist Charles Edwin Woodrow Bean won. He spent the war alongside Australian soldiers at Gallipoli, where he was wounded, and at the Western Front. After the war he was appointed Official War Historian.

exercise, ordering the other two brigades to make the journey on foot. It was a gruelling march, and though the 15th Brigade suffered in the extreme heat, it was the men of the 14th who endured the most. They were forced to march 65 kilometres in 40-degree heat carrying their full kit, which weighed about 40 kilograms. The march took three days. The men did not have enough water. They suffered from exhaustion, heat distress and dehydration and many collapsed by the roadside.

The Australian Army's Official War Historian, Captain Charles Bean, wrote that this episode was 'the harshest experience' of training ever. Major General McCay on the other hand, thought it was a very poor display and berated his men, saying that the 14th Brigade had to 'pull itself together'.

Learning How to Shoot

The new recruits were all **infantry** — they were foot soldiers. Like all soldiers, they had learned how to shoot a rifle, but the new divisions also needed **artillery** to support them. Men were needed to operate the heavy guns. There were a few men with experience but the artillery units were mostly made up of infantry and light-horse soldiers who volunteered to do artillery training. These new recruits had to be turned into skilled artillery operators in the shortest possible time.

There weren't enough trained officers to teach the 3,000 men that the divisions would need to operate the heavy guns, so the first job was to train the instructors. Training was conducted from 4.30 a.m. to 6.30 a.m. each morning. Then for the rest of the day, the instructors, with their new knowledge, would train the recruits.

To France

After three months training in Egypt, I ANZAC and II ANZAC were ordered to go to France. They boarded ships at Alexandria and in six days they were disembarking at Marseilles, a port in southern France. Finally they were on their way to the battlefront where they would fight for their country — where they would face the enemy.

This is what the men had been waiting for.

Chapter 2
Green Fields and Barbed Wire

28 June 1916, Steenbecque, France
Private Walter McAlister,
60th Battalion, 15th Brigade

I can't believe it. I'm in France! Sally would be green with envy. She's always dreamt of going to Europe, but instead, it's me who's here. Everything's so hush-hush they don't tell us exactly where we're going, but here we are in a village called Steenbecque.

You never heard such cheering as when we first caught sight of France on the horizon. As we sailed into the harbour at Marseilles, there was a lovely castle on the cliffs. Someone said it was where the Count of Monte Cristo was imprisoned. Imagine that! On the train from Marseilles I felt like I was in a storybook myself. The countryside was so beautiful, like a fairyland. The trees are a different sort of green to the trees at home, a brilliant green. And the fields are full of waving wheat and barley, sprinkled with the red of poppies and the blue of cornflowers. It's such a relief after the glaring light and blast-furnace heat of Egypt with its endless sand and flies. No flies in France, no mozzies either!

We spent three days and nights on the train — 15 men squashed into one compartment. They were all new recruits like me, except for one sergeant who was at Gallipoli. He's a bit of a sourpuss. The chaps are always having a joke and a laugh, but he never raises so much as a smile.

We passed through little villages that looked like they were paintings. The streets were cobbled, the houses were made of pale stone with red-tiled roofs. The roads that twisted through the fields from village to village were white, like they were all leading to Paradise. You can just feel the history in the air here. I saw beautiful old churches, cathedrals and a palace, which that Gallipoli sergeant told us was Versailles. The train stopped for a while just then, so we had a chance to really take it in. I've never seen such a big place!

And the people! They're so friendly, so welcoming. Every time the train stopped, there'd be a crowd of people waving and cheering us like we were the team that had just won the Grand Final. 'Vive l'Australie!' they shouted. Old women gave us flowers, and crucifixes to protect us. Young women gave us kisses! All we had to give them in return were tins of **bully beef**. *I thought I'd be able to write and tell Sally all about the French fashions, but the women don't worry much about fashion, not in this part of France anyway. Most of them just wear plain black dresses.*

We arrived last night and we're **billeted** *in a barn. A woman sold us eggs and butter and fresh bread and we all ignored our rations and cooked up a load of fried eggs on toast. What a treat! A young girl brought us coffee. It's like we're at the Ritz. Except that during the night the guns started up. They're miles away, but you can hear the roar of the artillery and feel the ground shake.*

This morning the sound of children laughing woke me and I got a look at our new digs. It's a pretty little farm, but there are a few dings in the buildings where they've been hit by **shells**. *The farm is busy. The whole family is out in the fields trying to carry on as if the war isn't a few miles from their door. Something isn't quite right. I can't put my finger on it.*

'There's no men.' It's that Gallipoli veteran — Sergeant Crawford. He's leaning on the barn wall having a smoke. It's like he's read my thoughts.

He's right. The whole time I've been in France all I've seen are women, children and old men. All the younger men are at war, every last one of them.

I go to the farmhouse to buy a few more eggs. Farmhouses are strange here — a big square of buildings with a gateway that leads into a courtyard. Sergeant

Crawford follows me. The old granny is the only one not out in the fields. She can't speak a word of English, but she understands my meaning. She invites me into the house. She's sewing, making dresses, black dresses, lots of them.

'That's all she does, day and night,' the sergeant says.

I don't grasp his meaning at first. I look at the pile of black dresses and the yards of black material waiting to be made into more. Then it hits me. The women are wearing black for a reason. There isn't one of them who hasn't lost someone in the war — husband, father, brother or son. They are all in mourning.

France couldn't have been more different to Egypt. It was summer, the fields were green, and the French people gave the Australian soldiers a warm welcome. Europe seemed civilised, and it was familiar to the Australians from their lessons at school. This was more like the experience the young men had been imagining.

'They pelted us with flowers and sweets and, while no one objected to the embraces of the girls, we thought it a bit too much when the men as well threw their arms around us and kissed us on both cheeks.'

Lieutenant Hugh Knyvett, 59th Battalion, 15th Brigade

An old French woman serves coffee to Australian and Scottish soldiers at an *estaminet* (small café) in her village, within 800 metres of the trenches.

AWM EZ0032

In France

Despite their long time in Egypt, the men of the Fifth Division conducted themselves well in Marseilles. A British colonel complimented them on their smart appearance, and the fact that not a single man was arrested for misbehaviour.

In military terms, a 'casualty' in a battle is any soldier who can no longer take part in combat. As well as those who are killed in action or die of wounds, it includes the wounded, those suffering from mental breakdowns and those taken prisoner by the enemy.

The train journey to the Western Front was like the sort of holiday none of the men would have been able to afford when they were civilians. Reality set in as the Australian soldiers marched towards the front line. The new recruits were excited at the thought of being involved in the war for the first time, but none of their training would in any way prepare them for life in the trenches.

The Nursery

At that time, the main battles of the war were taking place about 80 kilometres south in the Somme region, and 350 kilometres south-east at Verdun. The Australian soldiers were sent to the sector near the town of Armentières in the north of France, where there had only been fierce fighting on two occasions since the formation of the Western Front. It was what was known as a 'nursery' area — a place where inexperienced recruits could get used to life in the trenches, become familiar with being close to the battlefront, and gradually be introduced to taking part in real confrontations in the form of small raids on the Germans.

'...we must fight now, at once, in order to give help to our comrades fighting desperately in the south...however little we may be ready, or however difficult it may be, we should never forgive ourselves if we did not make the necessary effort and, if necessary, sacrifice, to help them.'

General Godley, General Officer Commanding, II ANZAC Corps, 7 July 1916

Bad News

The Battle of the Somme was a major **offensive** launched by the British and the French over a 30-kilometre front. It was intended to crush German forces. British generals had optimistically predicted that the battle would soon be won, but their confidence was misplaced. The opening day resulted in shocking British casualties. The Germans were proving to be more powerful than they had thought.

To make matters worse, the British had discovered, among the enemy dead, German soldiers from units that were supposed to be

At the beginning of World War I, German soldiers wore helmets called Pickelhaube *which were made of boiled leather and topped with a metal spike. At this time, Allied soldiers did not wear helmets at all. Both sides soon realised that trench warfare required soldiers to have good protection against head wounds. Steel helmets were issued to British soldiers in 1915. Australian soldiers received steel helmets in 1916, but at the time of the Battle of Fromelles about half the soldiers did not have helmets. The Germans found that the shiny metallic spike on the* Pickelhaube *made them an easy target for Allied snipers. Cloth helmet covers were issued, and then steel helmets were gradually introduced in 1916.*

A German recruitment poster showing a soldier with a cloth cover over his *Pickelhaube* helmet.

stationed further north. This confirmed that the German Army was sending soldiers from quieter sections of the Front to swell the numbers fighting at the Somme. The Fourth Australian Division was immediately sent to the Somme. Their time in the nursery had been short-lived.

General Haking, the British General who commanded the Allied forces in that sector, wanted the Fifth Division to conduct raids and attacks to occupy the Germans and stop them from sending more men to the Somme. He thought that the area around the village of Fromelles was a good place for such raids.

The three **brigades** of the Fifth Division — 8th, 14th and 15th — arrived at the Western Front to discover that 'the nursery' was about to become a battlefront — and they were to take part in the planned attack.

Chopping and Changing

General Haking put forward a plan for an attack on a German position called Aubers Ridge. He proposed that the Fifth Australian Division join two British divisions in a combined attack.

Haking's superiors rejected this plan, and instead of an attack, an artillery 'demonstration' was suggested. Allied big guns would fire at the German position for three days in a show of artillery strength. As it was to be merely a diversion, there would be no attempt to capture German-held ground.

Then the commanders changed their minds again and came up with a compromise of the two earlier plans. The attack was set for 17 July. Haking discovered that he did not have as much artillery as he thought, and the artillery units he did have were made up mainly of men who were under-trained and had no experience at all in the field. The amount of ammunition allocated for the battle was also well below what he had requested. He had to cut back his plans, reducing the fighting force to two divisions and narrowing the attack front.

'We had not been two days in the trenches before we knew that we were destined for an attack on the trenches opposite and we had not had time even to know the way about our own lines.'

Lieutenant Hugh Knyvett, 59th Battalion, 15th Brigade

The Fifth Division found themselves defending a stretch of the Western Front 1.8 kilometres long. Alongside them was the British Sixty-first Division, the other division that would be taking part in the battle. Though the soldiers of the Fifth Division were completely inexperienced, Major General McCay was very pleased that soldiers under his command would be the first Australians to take part in action on the Western Front.

Trenches

The purpose of the trenches was to protect the soldiers from enemy gunfire and grenades. A trench was about half a metre wide at the bottom and about two metres wide at the top, but it was the depth that was most important. The trench had to be deep enough to protect soldiers from enemy gunfire as they stood or moved about. For further protection, sandbags were piled up on the edge of the trench to create a barrier called a **parapet**. Though they were called sandbags, the canvas bags were actually filled with the muddy soil dug from the trenches. To make the parapet bulletproof, sandbags were stacked in rows up to six metres thick. The opposing armies hid from one another in their trenches, only raising their heads above the parapets when they were ordered to shoot at the enemy.

An unidentified Australian soldier sleeps in the trenches at Bois Grenier in the sector known as 'the nursery'.

AWM EZ0052

Soldiers fighting in Flanders struggle to move a field gun stuck in deep mud.

The ground in this area of France was very marshy. It was impossible for the soldiers to dig deep trenches because after digging down for a metre they would reach water. Digging a deep trench would have resulted in water at least knee-deep. So instead they dug shallow trenches with higher sandbag parapets. To keep the men's feet out of the muddy trench floor, wooden tracks called duckboards were laid. In many places the ground was so soggy the soldiers couldn't dig trenches at all, and they had to build thick walls of sandbags up to 2.5 metres high instead, which were known as breastworks.

*The trenches weren't always dug in straight lines. Ideally, they were built with notches consisting of two right-angle bends every 15 metres or so. These were called **traverses**. If the enemy could get guns in a position where they could fire down the length of a straight trench, the effects could be devastating. Traverses gave protection against this side-on fire (known as '**enfilade**') and from exploding grenades as well.*

A Bulge in the Line

Between the Allied and the German trenches was an area known as no-man's-land. Along the battlefront, no-man's-land was 450 metres at its widest, and 100 metres at its narrowest. Just beyond the trenches, each army erected wire entanglements so that the enemy couldn't easily get into their trenches if they did make it across no-man's-land. These wire entanglements consisted of rows of metal stakes hammered into the ground around which barbed wire was twisted and coiled.

At one point, near the town of Fromelles, the German front line bulged into no-man's-land. The Germans had built a strong concrete bunker on a slight rise in the ground and stationed machine gunners there. The countryside was so flat that even such a small prominence was a big advantage, turning the position into a fortress, which the Allies called the Sugar Loaf. The fact that it jutted out into no-man's-land meant that it provided the Germans with a good vantage point over Allied positions. If the battle was to be a success, the Allies would have to capture the Sugar Loaf.

The Allies called the bunker the 'Sugar Loaf' because its shape reminded them of a type of sweet bread that could be bought locally.

False Start

The men of the Fifth and the Sixty-first Divisions worked for two days and nights preparing for General Haking's attack, carrying tonnes of equipment to the front line trenches — ammunition, grenades, sandbags, scaling ladders and shovels. They created huge ammunition dumps behind the front line. Waterlogged trenches had to have new duckboards laid in them.

While the soldiers of the Fifth Division got used to the conditions at the Front, their commander, Major General McCay, set up his headquarters in Sailly Chateau, about eight kilometres behind the front line.

On the eve of the battle, the commander of I ANZAC, General Birdwood, was concerned about the wisdom of an attack using such inexperienced men and where preparation had been so rushed. He thought it should be cancelled. Brigadier General Elliott, commander of the 15th Brigade, also had grave concerns. But General Haking was confident of the plan's success, claiming that the men were ready for battle and any cancellation would be bad for morale.

The weather decided for them. In the early hours of the 17 July, a heavy mist lay over the area and the battle was postponed for two days. This gave the exhausted soldiers a chance to rest and revive themselves.

Over a 10-day period in early July, the plan of attack had changed six times.

The Final Plan

General Haking's plan was to capture 4,000 yards (3.6 kilometres) of the German front line opposite them. His tactics conformed to the standard plan of taking the enemy's trench — with one deviation. There would be no element of surprise, as the battle was to commence with a long artillery **bombardment**.

The plan was for the artillery-gunners to create a curtain of shell fire called a **barrage** aimed at the German trenches. After several hours, the gunners would then change the range of the guns and aim the barrage behind the trenches at the German artillery. This was standard procedure when an attack was about to be made. But there would be no immediate attack. The change of target was to be a **feint**, only intended to trick the Germans into thinking that an attack was about to take place. To make the fake attack even more convincing, Allied soldiers were instructed to raise their bayonets above the parapets and even to make dummy soldiers to hold up. The German soldiers, convinced that the Allies were about to attack, would man their parapets ready to take aim at them.

But Haking's plan for this battle was that the Allied artillery would instead suddenly aim their big guns back at the trenches and catch the Germans on their parapets. This was to happen every half hour for two hours, so that when the Allies did finally attack, the Germans would be expecting it to be a trick and wouldn't man the parapets.

Haking was confident that any German soldiers who hadn't been killed by the bombardment would be cowering in their bunkers. The Allied soldiers would then be able to charge across no-man's-land in relative safety and take the enemy front line trench.

First Battle

The three brigades of the Fifth Division were to attack side by side, but only two **battalions** from each brigade would make the initial assault. The third battalion would follow the attacking troops as a carrying party to transport all the required ammunition. The fourth battalion would be kept in reserve about 650 metres behind the front line, only to join the battle if General Haking gave specific orders.

'Finally, when we have cut all the wire, destroyed all the enemy's machine-gun emplacements, knocked down most of his parapets, killed a large proportion of the enemy, and thoroughly frightened the remainder, our infantry will assault, capture and hold the enemy's support line along the whole front.'

General Haking, General Officer Commanding, 16 July 1916

The assaulting troops would attack in four waves at five-minute intervals, with the soldiers advancing about 1.8 metres apart. Aerial photographs had identified a second and third line of trenches behind the German front line. Once they had taken the front line trench, the Allied soldiers were then to take the second trench behind it, finally making their own new front line in the third trench about 150 metres behind the German front line.

While this was all happening, each brigade had to dig two trenches across no-man's-land so that there could be safe movement into the German trenches once they had been captured. Trenches at each end of the captured line would be dug across no-man's-land to join the new section to the original front line on either side. On paper it all looked simple.

'None of these divisions would have been ordered fit for present use in the Somme offensive, the Fifth Australian being too new, the Sixty-first a numerically weak Territorial division recently arrived from England...'

Captain C E W Bean, Official Australian War Historian

The men of the Fifth Division were finally going to do what they had joined the army to do. The coming battle would be the first battle on the Western Front for Australian soldiers. As it turned out, the least experienced Australian troops were going to take part in it.

Chapter 3
Lethal Weapons

18 July 1916, Fleurbaix Sector, Western Front, France
Private Walter McAlister,
60th Battalion, 15th Brigade

We're in the front line. Our first time. I've never been so exhausted in my life, but now we've finally got a chance to rest. We scraped shallow recesses in the side of the trench, wrapped ourselves in our greatcoats, used our packs as pillows. The others all went out like a light, but I can't get to sleep. It's the guns. The sound of the heavy guns.

They make a particular noise when they're fired. Crump, crump. *It's like no other sound you've ever heard. It's distant, but the ground shakes. There's a whizzing sound and you hold your breath to see if the shell's going to land on you. Then there's another and another.*

Sometimes it's our big guns, sometimes it's theirs. Then there'll be a silence. That's why I can't sleep. I'm just lying here waiting for the next one. It doesn't seem to bother the other blokes. I know Fritz is aiming at our guns, which are miles away. It's unlikely we'll get hit, but you never know.

We started off at dusk, marching in our companies 200 yards apart. It was a beautiful French summer evening. I could hear the last calls of birds as they noisily settled down for the night. It's been a while since we made a long march, and the cobblestones were hard on the feet. No one dared fall out though, no matter how sore their feet were.

After a couple of miles, we stopped for a break, and everyone was quiet, sensing that the enemy was close. Then we were divided into our platoons. They were worried that Fritz might notice a big group of blokes from their observation posts.

We left the road and the hedges behind and walked across a wheat field. I felt exposed, which was stupid because the hedges wouldn't have protected us from gunfire. We divided into our sections, just ten men.

Then suddenly the path sloped and we were in a trench, with the sandbag parapets towering over our heads. I should have been relieved that we had some protection, but the sudden darkness and the narrowness was suffocating. The trench smelt of mud and explosives and urine and decay. It was a communication trench leading to the front line trenches, but not in a straight line. Communication trenches zig-zag back and forth, so that if a shell hits, it lessens the damage.

Then the heavy guns started up. Not ours, theirs. The earth shook and the shells were landing close.

'Keep moving,' said the section leader. 'They're not aiming at us.'

You could have fooled me.

Then there was a whiz and an ear-splitting bang and I was lifted clean off my feet, thrown back about five yards. Earth rained down on me. I sat up. My ears were ringing and I couldn't believe I was still in one piece.

In front of us, instead of the trench, there was a huge shell hole. A man was lying up on what was left of the parapet. It was Bish. His eyes were wide open like he was surprised to see us. His arms and legs were intact, but flung about like he was a discarded rag doll. I couldn't see any wounds. There was no blood, but I knew for sure he was dead. He was just a slab of meat. That was the first time I'd seen a dead person, and I'd been sharing a **dixie** *of tea with him not 20 minutes before. I got to my feet. There were lots of dead men, their bodies mutilated, and others who weren't dead, but bleeding, screaming, wishing they were.*

It hit me that I could be dead by tomorrow. I didn't even think about it. My feet were scrambling up the other side of the ruined trench.

*'***Latrine***,' I heard myself saying.*

I just wanted to get away to somewhere safe. I crawled back through the wheat field on my hands and knees, so no one could see me. It was dark by then. I didn't have a plan. I didn't know where I was going, but I knew I wasn't going to the front. I didn't care how many white feathers I got. I didn't care if I ended up in jail. I am a coward. And that's why, when I came to another trench, I dived into it. I tried to look like I had an urgent message to deliver.

Then a hand grabbed my shoulder.

'Where do you think you're going, private?'

It was Sergeant Crawford. I'd lost my way in the field and looped back to the communication trench.

'I can't...' That's all I managed to say.

'You can.' He was still gripping my shoulder. He leaned in close to me. 'You must,' he whispered. 'Otherwise I'll have to hand you over to the **Provosts**. *I should do that anyway, but you'll be* **court-martialled**. *You wouldn't want to disgrace your family would you?'*

I thought of Mum working in a clothing factory, Billy going home to an empty house after school. I thought of Sally. She'd never speak to me again.

'Come on, son.'

I followed him back to my **company**.

There are rats. I can see them trying to get into our tucker bags, scraping away at tins to get the last scraps of bully beef. They're big buggers. Someone said that's because they eat the dead. There are bodies out in no-man's-land and the rats eat their flesh and gnaw on their bones. I don't know whether that's true or not. The guns are quiet at last, but I still can't sleep.

In earlier times, the main thrust of a battle was a charge. Men from opposing sides, on foot and on horseback, would charge at each other across open ground, meeting with a clash of hand-held weapons — spears, swords, and later, guns. The soldiers of both sides were equally at risk of being killed.

Guns of All Sizes

On the Western Front, British generals still believed that the only way to win a battle was for the infantry to charge at the enemy, but in trench warfare, a charge had become a lop-sided affair. The attackers had to climb out of the shelter of their trenches and cross no-man's-land where they were in the direct line of fire from an enemy shooting at them from the safety of their trenches.

In trench warfare an attacking force could suffer up to 14 times the number of casualties as the defenders.

World War I weapons were guns of all sizes — those in the hands of the soldiers, larger guns carried onto the battlefield by a team of men, and the big guns which stayed in one place behind the battlefield.

Small Arms

The guns carried by infantry soldiers are called small arms. In World War I, every soldier was issued with a bolt-action rifle that had an effective firing range of almost half a kilometre. He also carried a bayonet — a blade that fitted onto the barrel of the rifle to turn it into a stabbing weapon for use in hand-to-hand fighting.

SMLE Rifle

At Fromelles, Allied soldiers used the SMLE rifle. This rifle was shorter than earlier models; **cartridges** were loaded ten at a time in a small metal case called a magazine; the firing mechanism was invented by a man called James Lee; and the guns were made at a factory in Enfield, on the outskirts of London. The rifle was therefore known as the Short Magazine Lee Enfield or SMLE. A trained soldier could fire between 10 and 15 cartridges in a minute.

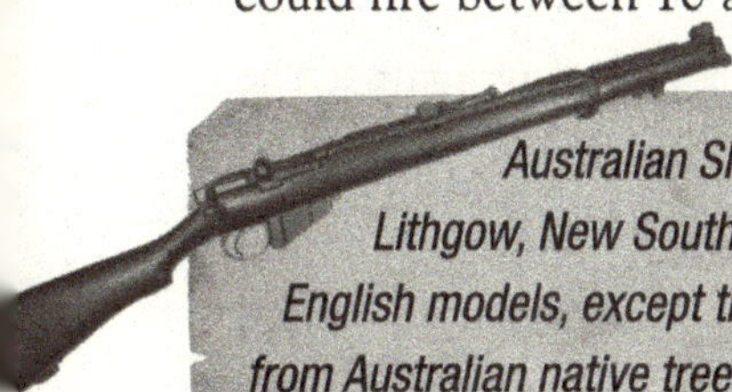

Australian SMLE rifles were made in a factory in Lithgow, New South Wales. The rifle was identical to the English models, except that the stock was made of wood from Australian native trees instead of the wood of the walnut tree.

AWM REL19280

Gewehr 98

German infantry soldiers were issued with a Mauser Gewehr 98. *Mauser* is the name of the manufacturer, *Gewehr* is the German word for rifle, and 98 refers to the year 1898 when the first model was made. This rifle was longer than the British rifles, and its firing rate was slower because the magazine held only five cartridges.

Hand Grenades

Infantry soldiers were also issued with grenades, which are small **bombs** that are thrown at enemy soldiers or equipment. Grenades could be carried safely by soldiers until activated by pulling a pin or ring. Detonation of the explosive material inside was delayed by a time fuse, giving the soldier a few seconds to throw it before it exploded.

Mills Bomb

British and Australian soldiers used an egg-shaped grenade made of cast iron. After the safety pin was removed, the Mills Bomb had an added safety feature. As long as the soldier gripped the grenade so that the striker lever lay against the body of the bomb, it would not explode. Once the soldier let go of the grenade, the striker lifted and set off a safety fuse, which allowed five seconds before the explosive charge inside the bomb exploded. The segmented casing of the grenade was designed to shatter when it exploded, sending out fragments of metal that could rip into flesh.

Earlier in the war, the British were manufacturing inadequate numbers of grenades; nothing like enough for the needs of trench warfare. Soldiers in the trenches had to make their own improvised grenades out of jam tins filled with dynamite and bits of metal or stones.

Stielhandgranate

The Germans mainly used *Stielhandgranate* or 'stick bombs'. These were cylindrical bombs about ten centimetres long screwed onto a wooden handle. They were activated by removing a screw cap at the bottom of the handle and pulling a ceramic ring inside. This triggered a six-second time fuse. Once the ring was pulled, the grenade had to be thrown immediately.

Machine Guns

Machine guns could be carried onto the battlefield, but required a team of at least six men to carry the gun and its tripod, set it up, and fire it. The ammunition was fed into the gun on a canvas belt which held 250 cartridges. The machine gun fired continuously for as long as the operator had his finger on the trigger and the cartridge belt still had cartridges.

A German MG 08 machine gun.

Machine guns were the most up-to-date gun technology in World War I and neither side had many. The loss of a machine gun, especially if it was captured in working order by the enemy, was a serious event. The machine guns used by the Allies and the Germans, the Vickers and the MG 08, were similar, both heavy and water cooled. This meant that machine-gunners had to carry water as well as ammunition.

The Lewis machine gun was introduced into Allied armies early in 1916. It was much lighter and could fire quicker than the Vickers, but the circular magazine mounted on the top of the gun held only 47 cartridges, so time was lost in reloading, which resulted in a similar firing rate to the Vickers. The Lewis had the added advantage of being air cooled, so soldiers operating it didn't have to carry a supply of water.

At the beginning of the war, the German Army had only 1,600 machine guns. By July 1916, they had 11,000.

World War I Machine Guns

Name	Weight	Range	Firing rate per minute	Crew
Allied machine guns				
Vickers	23 kg	2 km	500	3
Lewis	15 kg	3 km	500	1
German machine guns				
MG 08	26.5 kg	2 km	500	4

Trench Mortars

A mortar is a more modern version of a cannon, designed to fire bombs at the enemy. They were used in the trenches rather than at the rear with the big guns. The bombs were loaded directly into the barrel and then fired in a high arc over a relatively short distance. This meant that soldiers, from the safety of their trenches, could fire the shells high and they could fall on the enemy trenches from above.

'The air was thick with bullets, swishing in a flat, criss-crossed lattice of death…Men were cut in two by streams of bullets.'
Private W H Downing, 57th Battalion, 15th Brigade

Soldiers who lived long enough learned to recognise the distinctive 'plop' sound of a mortar being fired from the trenches opposite, and then would watch the skies for the approaching shell. If it looked like it was going to land on them, they would get out of the way as fast as possible.

A bullet is a metal projectile fired from a gun such as a pistol, rifle or machine gun. A cartridge contains the bullet and the explosive in a metal casing. When the weapon is fired, the explosive makes the bullet shoot out, and the casing stays behind to be ejected from the gun. A shell is fired from a large artillery gun. It contains high explosive or ***shrapnel****.*

At the beginning of the war, the Allies did not have any mortars to counter the German mortars which were called *Minenwerfer*. In just a few months, an English inventor called Wilfred Stokes devised a trench mortar that was simpler, lighter and more efficient than the Minenwerfer. It broke down into barrel, base plate and stand so that a team of three men could carry it.

'There was the frightful chaos of Minenwerfers, shaking the ground into waves, trailing lines of sparks crisscrossed on the gloom, swerving just before they fell, confounding, dreadful, abhorred far more than shells, killing many by their very ***concussion****, destroying all within yards.'*

Private W H Downing, 57th Battalion, 15th Brigade

World War I Trench Mortars

Name	Weight	Range	Size of Shell	Crew
Allied Trench Mortars				
Stokes light mortar	47 kg	700 m	4.5 kg	3
2-inch medium mortar	48 kg	500 m	23 kg	5
9.45-inch heavy mortar	227 kg	2 km	69 kg	7
German Trench Mortars				
25-cm Minenwerfer	768 kg	900 m	97 kg	6
17-cm Minenwerfer	483 kg	800 m	50 kg	5
7.58-cm Minenwerfer	163 kg	300 m	4.6 kg	5

Though the barrel of a medium trench mortar was only 50 milimetres in diameter, the spherical bomb that it fired was 230 mm. They were mounted on shafts, and the shafts were loaded into the barrel, with the bomb sticking out the top. These bombs were nicknamed 'toffee apples'. The bombs of the heavy trench mortars were known as 'flying pigs'.

An Australian trench mortar class, Lahoussoye, France. The soldiers are receiving instructions on the operation of a Stokes mortar.

AWM E00066

Artillery

Larger free-standing guns are referred to as artillery, and classified as light or heavy. In World War I, they fired shells, weighing from less than half a kilo to more than half a tonne, at high speed. Mounted on carriages and towed into position by teams of horses, these guns were placed five to ten kilometres behind the actual battle. The gunners couldn't see where their shells were landing; the victims never saw the gun that killed or wounded them.

The shells were filled with either high explosives or small balls of lead called shrapnel. Shrapnel shells exploded in flight above the heads of enemy soldiers. High explosive shells exploded on impact, and a single shell was capable of destroying metres of trenches, blowing up buildings and big guns, and killing many enemy soldiers.

At the Battle of Fromelles, the Allies had about three times as many guns as the Germans.

Howitzers are cannons that have shorter barrels, lower velocity and shorter range than other artillery. The howitzers used in World War I could fire shells about twice the weight of a similar-sized field gun. The shells were fired in a high arc so they could hit targets behind parapets, walls or hills. They were differentiated by the diameter of their shells, for example, 9.2 inches.

A British World War I recruitment poster.

Artillery at the Battle of Fromelles

Name	Weight	Range	Size of shell	Crew	Estimated No. at Fromelles
Allied Artillery					
18-pounder	1.25 tonnes	6 km	8.4 kg	6	210
60-pounder	4.5 tonnes	9 km	27 kg	10	36
4.5-inch howitzer	1.3 tonnes	6.5 km	16 kg	6	64
6-inch howitzer	3.7 tonnes	8 km	45 kg	10	22
9.2-inch howitzer	12 tonnes	9 km	132 kg	14	8
German Artillery					
Feldkanone 96 n/A	1 tonne	11 km	6.8 kg	6	73
10.5 cm leFH 18 howitzer	2 tonnes	10 km	14.8 kg	5	29

Taking Aim

When an artillery unit is ordered to fire its heavy guns all at once, it is called a bombardment. The bombardment that opened the Battle of Fromelles had three functions. Firstly, the gunners went through a process called 'registration'. This was, in effect, a sort of target practice. The guns were fired and observers with binoculars got as close as they could to the target and watched where the shells landed.

Then they telephoned back to the gunners to tell them if they had fallen short or over shot. The gunners would then adjust the angle and direction of the gun barrel, and the strength of the charge and try again until they hit the target.

The bombardment was also supposed to destroy the enemy's wire entanglements so that Allied soldiers could reach the enemy trenches. Finally the bombardment was aimed at the enemy's front line trenches in order to kill as many German soldiers as possible, so that the Allies could take the German trenches without sustaining many casualties themselves.

Other Equipment

An Australian soldier going into battle carried only what was absolutely necessary — 120 rounds of ammunition for his rifle, some food rations (a tin of bully beef and some hard biscuits), a water bottle, two grenades and two empty sandbags for building new

During the bombardments at the opening of the Battle of the Somme, the guns were loud enough to be heard across the English Channel, as far away as London, where the vibrations rattled teacups 260 kilometres from the battlefield.

parapets. This equipment was known as battle order. Each soldier also carried a small medical kit. For identification he wore identity discs, and in his pocket he carried his pay book.

At the Battle of Fromelles, every third man carried a pick or a shovel for digging trenches.

'How many guns we had at work I do not know...hundreds... thousands...but they all began at once...hurricanes, whirlwinds, thunderstorms and gigantic conflagrations: bring them altogether and concentrate them all in a ring of a few acres, and you have only a faint idea of what went on immediately before our eyes.'

Lance Corporal E A Hubbard,
53rd Battalion, 14th Brigade

Under-prepared

The most experienced soldiers had been sent to the Somme. None of the divisions left around Fromelles were considered ready for such a fight. A large proportion of the Fifth Division was inexperienced, the Sixty-first was depleted, having only two-thirds of its regular number of soldiers.

The artillery was as under-prepared as the infantry. Men who had been infantrymen or members of the Australian Light Horse a few months earlier, were now about to take part in their first battle as artillery men. Additional artillery was borrowed from other British divisions.

Two trench mortar batteries were also borrowed for the battle, as well as Canadian mortar operators to take the place of the inexperienced Australians, who were relegated to the role of assistants.

Chapter 4
Attack

19 July 1916, Fleurbaix Sector, Western Front, France
Private Walter McAlister,
60th Battalion, 15th Brigade

The guns have been going all day long. It's enough to drive you crazy — the constant deafening roar, the shriek of a shell as it heads our way, the waiting to see if this is going to be the shell that blows you to pieces. Only seconds, but it seems like ages. Then there's a thud and an ear-splitting bang as it hits. Further down the line the 8th got hit pretty bad. We've been lucky.

'We're charmed,' Thommo says. 'Nothing will touch us today. With a bit of luck, I'll get a little smack in the arm or the leg. Just enough to get me a ***Blighty****.'*

It's only an hour till ***zero hour****. I'm terrified. None of the other men seem scared at all. Some of them are joking, lounging back against the sandbags and smoking like* *they're in the pub. One man is reading his New Testament. A couple of them are re-reading letters from home.*

Sarge handed out letters this morning, while we were having breakfast. It was the best breakfast I'd had since I'd been in the army — eggs, bacon, a big hunk of fresh bread.

'The condemned man's last meal,' one of the men said.

Everyone laughed. I didn't think it was funny.

I think Sarge saved the letters till this morning, so we had something to cheer us up. Make us remember why we're here. I got one from Mum. I didn't want to open it in front of the others. Mum's gone all religious since I've been in the army. She sends me these Bible verses that she's written out and decorated with pressed flowers from our garden. The other chaps would laugh if they saw them, so I put the letter in my pocket unopened.

One of the other blokes stands up on the **fire step** *and looks over the parapet. He could get his head blown off, but he doesn't.*

'The artillery's doing its job,' he says. 'Fritz's trenches are getting blown to pieces.'

Everyone cheers.

I'm just about to open my letter, when next thing I know, word is passed along that the first wave is going over in five minutes. I stuff the letter back in my pocket. I put on my slouch hat. There were only enough tin helmets for the first two waves and I'm in the fourth wave. There's no joking now. This is it.

'Over you go,' says our battalion commander, Major McCrae, and the first wave jumps up on the fire step and leaps over the sandbags as one man. Over goes the next wave. No one hesitates. They could be kids playing a game. I can see the major at the end of the line. He's going over with the last wave, with us. His promotion to lieutenant colonel hasn't gone through yet, so he's still a major. He's a good bloke. He'll see us right.

Then I'm jumping over the sandbags. I feel like someone else is making my body work. I can see the gap cut in our wire and I run through it. I'm in no-man's-land. It looks like a place where children should be playing — long grass waving in the breeze, wild flowers, the remains of an orchard. I can see green apples on the branches.

We run through the grass in the evening sunlight. I have to wade through a ditch full of water. It'll be all right, I think. It's not as bad as I thought it would be. The smoke clears a bit, but I can't see the first waves of men in front of us, just the swaying grass. Major McCrae is on my right. He's still striding on, so I do too.

I can just hear another sound under the roar of the heavy guns. It's the rat-a-tat of machine guns. Machine gun bullets are suddenly thick in the air. Major McCrae stops in his tracks, like he's just remembered something important. Then he crumples to the ground and disappears beneath the grass. I trip over something. It's a body. One of my battalion. I crawl along and amid the grass there are bodies everywhere. Lots of them. Men I know. I flatten myself against the earth, wriggling like a snake. Machine-gun bullets skim above me or smack into the earth. One goes through the sleeve of my jacket, but somehow misses my arm.

The machine-gun fire gets heavier. I see a shell hole and I tumble into it. I can hear rasping breathing and low moans. I'm not the only one who's taken refuge here. There are five others. Three of ours and two from the 59th. Their uniforms are dark with blood. They have terrible wounds. I see a hand hanging by a thread of skin, a head with only half a face, fingers holding a stomach with a mangled length of intestine visible through them. At least three of the men are dead.

I should be shocked, I should feel sick, but instead I want to sing.

I'm alive.

THE 19TH OF July is a sunny day. The soldiers of the Fifth Division are given a better than usual breakfast. Those that aren't already in the front line prepare to march in from their billets to the front line trenches. They are in good spirits despite the fact that they are about to take part in their first battle. For some of them it will also be their last.

The Combatants

The Australians

Fifth Australian Division
General Officer Commanding: Major General McCay

Brigades	8th	14th	15th
Brigade Commander	Brigadier General Tivey	Colonel Pope	Brigadier General Elliott
Attacking Battalions	32nd, 31st	54th, 53rd	60th, 59th
Battalion Commanders	Lieutenant Colonel Coghill, Lieutenant Colonel Toll	Lieutenant Colonel Cass, Lieutenant Colonel Norris	Major McCrae, Lieutenant Colonel Harris
Reserve Battalions	29th, 30th	55th, 56th	57th, 58th

The British

Sixty-first Division
General Officer Commanding: Major General McKenzie

Brigades	184th	183rd	182nd
Brigade Commander	Brigadier General Carter	Brigadier General Stewart	Brigadier General Gordon
Assault Battalions	2/1st Buckinghamshire, 2/4th Royal Berkshire	2/4th Gloucestershire, 2/6th Gloucestershire	2/6th Royal Warwickshire, 2/7th Royal Warwickshire
Reserve Battalions	2/5th Gloucestershire 2/1st Buckinghamshire	2/7th Worcestershire, 2/8th Worcestershire	2/5th Royal Warwickshire, 2/8th Royal Warwickshire

The Germans

Sixth Bavarian Reserve Division
Commander: Lieutenant General Gustav Scanzoni von Lichtenfels

Regiments	21st Bavarian Reserve Infantry Regiment	16th Bavarian Reserve Infantry Regiment	17th Bavarian Reserve Infantry Regiment
Battalions	3rd	3rd	3rd
Companies	10, 11, 12	9, 10, 11	10

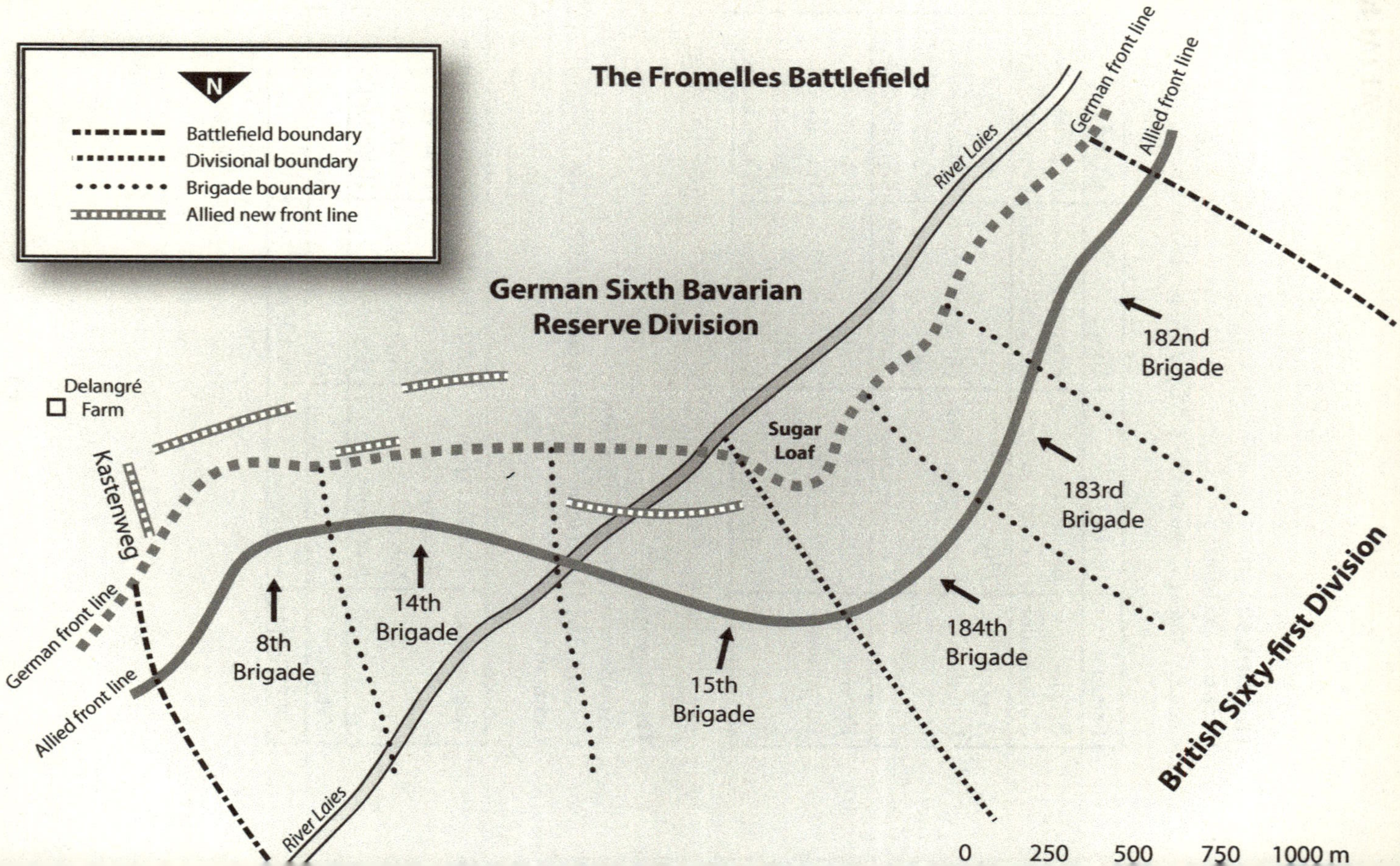
The Fromelles Battlefield
N
Battlefield boundary
Divisional boundary
Brigade boundary
Allied new front line
German Sixth Bavarian Reserve Division
Delangré Farm
Kastenweg
River Laies
River Laies
German front line
Allied front line
German front line
Allied front line
Sugar Loaf
8th Brigade
14th Brigade
15th Brigade
184th Brigade
183rd Brigade
182nd Brigade
British Sixty-first Division
0 250 500 750 1000 m

11 a.m.

The Allied artillery bombardment begins. The Germans retaliate with half-hearted rifle fire.

New steel helmets have been issued to the Australian soldiers, but there aren't enough for everyone. The soldiers who will be in the first two waves all get helmets, but many of those in the third and fourth waves just wear their slouch hats.

'Today I lead my battalion in an assault on the German lines and I pray to God I may come through all right and bring honour to our name. If not I will at least have laid down my life for you and my country, which is the greatest privilege one can ask for.'

Major Geoff McCrae, 60th Battalion Commander, 15th Brigade, letter to his family 19 July 1916

1 p.m.

The Allied artillery now adjust their settings and aim their shells to cut the Germans' wire entanglements. News spreads among the waiting men that their artillery is successfully doing its job. But the artillery observers know that only some sections of the German wire entanglement have been cut and that the all-important Sugar Loaf has not been damaged. There are still hours of bombardment to go, so they are not concerned about this.

'...almost between the divisions lay the Sugar Loaf, a sinister and terrible place, crowded with concrete emplacements...'

Lieutenant Colonel C MacLaurin, Australian Army Medical Corps

In a battle, the points of the compass are not used to indicate directions. Whichever way the army is attacking is forward, behind them is to the rear. The other directions are left and right.

Men of the 53rd Battalion a few minutes before the attack at Fromelles.

AWM H16396

2 p.m.

The Germans strike back. Their big guns are aimed at the areas just behind the Allied lines where the soldiers are assembling. One of the 8th Brigade's ammunition dumps is hit by an enemy shell, causing a massive explosion that kills signallers, messengers and medical staff. Lieutenant Colonel Toll, one of their battalion commanders, is wounded in the head.

3 p.m.

The Allied artillery-gunners readjust the angle of their guns and aim behind enemy lines. This is supposed to trick the Germans into thinking that the Allies are about to attack. The gunners then quickly aim back at the trenches, hoping to catch the enemy soldiers as they take positions on their parapets. The Germans don't take the bait.

The German shelling increases in intensity. To make matters worse, men of the 8th Brigade on the far left of the attack front, where no-man's-land is at its narrowest, are hit by shells from their own big guns that have fallen short. The inexperienced artillery men haven't yet learned to set their range accurately.

At 3.30 p.m. the men of the 15th Brigade are the first Australian soldiers in position in the front line trenches on the right of the Australian position. Fifteen minutes later, the 14th Brigade is in position in the centre.

4 p.m.

The 8th Brigade gets into position on the far left, as the artillery again lift their barrage to make the Germans think an Allied attack is about to begin. Half an hour later, they repeat the process. To the right of the Australians, the British troops are also getting ready for the battle.

The officers who will lead the Australian battalions onto the battlefield are in the trenches with their men. The brigade commanders are several kilometres behind the lines, except for Brigadier General Elliott who is in charge of the 15th Brigade. He wants to be closer to the action and is 300 metres behind the front line trench. Major General McCay, the commander of the Fifth Division, and General Haking, the battle commander, have both set up their battle headquarters about six kilometres away. General Haig, the commander-in-chief of the entire war, is more than 20 kilometres behind the lines.

The enemy's fire increases and is now aimed at the Allied front line. The 8th Brigade is the worst hit. The casualties are so high that their third and fourth waves have to be combined. Hundreds of men have already been killed or wounded, and the battle hasn't even started. Rumours spread among the Australian soldiers that spies must have informed the enemy of the battle plan, as they seem to know exactly what the Allies are doing.

5 p.m.

The Allied artillery stages their final barrage lift. By this time it is hoped that the Germans are expecting the fake attack and not a real one. But things are not going to plan.

Zero hour for the battle is 6 p.m., but the Australian soldiers start 'hopping the bags' at 5.45 p.m. so they can get into position. The battle has begun. Elliott tells the 15th Brigade that the artillery has been successful and they won't face any resistance. The first wave of his men leap over the parapet with confidence, even though they have the widest stretch of no-man's-land to cross and they are closest to the Sugar Loaf. It is quiet for a minute or two. Then they are met with a 'veritable blizzard of bullets'. Few of them escape death or wounding.

'Boys, you won't find a German in those trenches when you get there.'

Brigadier General Harold Elliott, 15th Brigade Commander

The next wave suffers a similar fate. When the third wave crosses the parapet they expect to see the other waves ahead, but there is no sign of them. They assume that their comrades are crouched in shell holes ready to make a final assault, but soon discover that most of the first two waves are lying dead or wounded, hidden by the grass. Many men of the third wave are also killed.

On the far left of the attack front, the 8th Brigade charges across their narrow stretch of no-man's-land. Their losses are high, but they reach the German front line in just 15 minutes. On the right, the British troops begin their attack.

6 p.m.

The fourth wave of the 15th Brigade emerges from the trenches, and with them the two battalion commanders. One is killed almost immediately. The British 184th Brigade on their right should have disabled the Sugar Loaf, but the soldiers of the 15th Brigade discover to their dismay that it is still intact and machine guns are still in operation. Men are dropping to the ground by the dozen, mown down by the lethal machine-gun fire. When the survivors get in sight of the enemy front line, they see that it is still manned with German soldiers.

'Hundreds were mown down in the flicker of an eyelid, like great rows of teeth knocked from a comb, but still the line went on…'
Private W H Downing, 57th Battalion, 15th Brigade

The 15th Brigade's telephone wires have been destroyed by shells and the air is thick with dust and smoke, so even though Brigadier General Elliott is in the front line trenches, he doesn't know how the attack is going. When the German rifle fire dies down, Elliott convinces himself that it is because his men have reached the enemy lines and all the Germans have been killed or driven away. In actual fact, the Germans have stopped firing because there are no 15th Brigade soldiers left for them to shoot at.

'Now came the sight I saw and it will live with me forever. The first sight I saw on ascending was the man in front of me blown to atoms, and then on the ground hundreds of my mates dead and wounded.'

Corporal Richard St John Kennedy, 32nd Battalion, 8th Brigade

When the soldiers of the 8th Brigade reach the German front line on the left, they are pleased to see enemy soldiers running away from them towards Delangré Farm, which is a German stronghold. There are Allied casualties, but the soldiers of the 8th kill or take prisoner the Germans remaining in the trenches.

Meanwhile, in the centre of the Australian battlefront, the 14th Brigade has also made it across no-man's-land. Their casualties are relatively light as they are out of the line of fire of the murderous Sugar Loaf machine guns. Their stretch of the German front line has been destroyed. They overcome the remaining Germans in hand-to-hand fighting. The Australian soldiers are amazed at the arrangements in the German front line. There are concrete shelters, and deep dugouts where German soldiers can shelter unharmed from the Allied barrage. Lieutenant Colonel Cass, one of the 14th's battalion commanders, sets up his headquarters in one of the shelters that is fitted with electric light and an armchair!

The orders are to occupy the third line of German trenches, so, under constant fire, the soldiers of the 8th and the 14th continue deeper into enemy territory, searching for these trenches. One of the 14th's battalion commanders, Lieutenant Colonel Norris, is killed by machine-gun fire. Twenty-one-year-old Captain Arblaster discovers that he is the most senior officer left alive in this battalion and therefore he is now in command.

The Allies still can't find the second line of German trenches, let alone the third. All they find are shallow, water-logged ditches. After walking 300 metres or more into enemy territory, they realise that there has been a mistake. The lines seen on the aerial photographs are not trenches, just ditches. There are no second and third line trenches.

6.30 p.m.

Lieutenant Colonel Toll is still in command of his battalion despite his wounds. He reports back to divisional headquarters that he is about 200 metres behind enemy lines and hasn't yet found the second line. His telephone lines have been cut during the battle, so he has to send the message by carrier pigeon.

Since there are no third-line trenches, the 14th and 8th Brigades attempt to turn the watery ditches into trenches that will become part of the new Allied front line. In water half a metre deep, soldiers fill their sandbags with sticky mud to create a soggy parapet.

Though the left and the centre brigades have achieved their first objective, on the right, the 15th Brigade's situation is bad. Out of 39 officers who hopped the bags, 35 are dead or wounded. A few men stagger back to the Australian lines to report that the scattered remains of their battalion are still out in no-man's-land. But Brigadier General Elliott clings to the belief that, since no one from the second battalion has returned, they at least must have reached the German front line. In fact, most of them are lying dead in no-man's-land. Having received news of the success of the 8th and the 14th, Elliott sends a messenger out to his remaining men in no-man's-land. They must make another assault on the German trenches.

'...a shell struck the top of the parapet with a terrific explosion. Two boys standing alongside of me started to cry for their mother and I told them to cut that out, but pray to god to get them out of this hole.'

Private William Barry, 31st Battalion, 8th Brigade

The 14th Brigade assumes that the 15th Brigade is occupying the German trench to their right. They don't know yet that the 15th Brigade has failed to reach the German trenches, and that the entire British attack has failed. The bombardment didn't destroy the German trenches and machine gun emplacements, so the British brigades have been met with devastating machine-gun fire. Few British soldiers made it to the German front line, and those that did did not survive for long.

Captain Arblaster's battalion is now on the right **flank** of the battle and has to defend itself against gunfire from the front and the side.

7 p.m.

In his headquarters, the battle commander, General Haking, gets news that the 8th and the 14th Brigades have taken the enemy front line trenches. He believes that some British soldiers have succeeded. Though he has no evidence, Brigadier General Elliott has also reported that one of the 15th's battalions has been successful. Haking believes the battle is going well, but it isn't.

Though the 8th and the 14th Brigades are taking up positions behind the previous enemy lines as ordered, there is a gap between them. They are not in communication with each other. Their flanks are exposed to German fire. Unable to find the second line of German trenches, Lieutenant Colonel Toll's battalion retraces its steps and takes up position in the empty German front line trench. This makes the new Australian front line even more disjointed.

On the left flank of the battlefront, the 8th Brigade discovers a well-built communication trench known as the Kastenweg leading from the German front line deeper into enemy territory. They drive the remaining Germans out of it and man the trench so that the left flank of the battlefront is secure.

Brigadier General Elliott learns that the British have failed to take the Sugar Loaf. Though there is success on the left, the attack on the right consisting of the 15th Brigade and all the British brigades has failed. The German gunners stationed in the Sugar Loaf are still spraying deadly machine-gun fire over the battlefield.

8 p.m.

Major General McCay authorises the reserve battalions to join the battle to reinforce the depleted attack battalions. The German gunners hit two ammunition dumps behind Allied lines. This reduces the amount of ammunition and creates a pall of smoke that drifts across the battlefield and makes it even harder for the soldiers digging in behind enemy lines to know where the others are. It does however provide a useful screen as Allied soldiers carry machine guns across no-man's-land to the new front line.

Brigadier General Elliott receives a request from the commander of the British 184th Brigade asking for support in a new attack on the Sugar Loaf that is due to take place at 9 p.m.

Meanwhile, General Haking has finally realised that the initial attack has failed. He cancels the 9 p.m. attack and orders the British troops to withdraw from the battlefield so that they can regroup.

Though the message about the cancelled attack reaches Fifth Division headquarters by 8.35 p.m., no word of it reaches Brigadier General Elliott. He organises his reserves to make the attack.

9 p.m.

Darkness is falling. On the dot of 9 p.m., the reserve battalion of the 15th Brigade leaps over the parapet and dashes across no-man's-land. A few survivors of the original attacking battalions rise up from the shell holes of no-man's-land and join them. They charge the left flank of the Sugar Loaf. All their commanders are dead, so they are led by 22-year-old Major Hutchinson.

What they don't know is that they are the only battalion to make the assault.

Chapter 5 The Dead and the Dying

19 July 1916, Fleurbaix Sector, Western Front, France
Private Walter McAlister,
60th Battalion, 15th Brigade

I am lying in this shell hole with three dead men to keep me company. I do what I can for the two who are still alive — drip iodine on their wounds, give them a sip of water, mutter useless words of comfort. It's getting dark. All I have to do is lie here till it's all over. I can pretend I got **shell shock**. *Then I can carry back these two wounded men. I might be a coward, but I can do that at least.*

I take out the photo of Sally that I keep in my breast pocket. There she is looking lovely in a pale dress with her hair loose. Mum's unopened letter is there, too. I pull the single sheet of paper from the envelope and three paper angels fall out. They are wearing long white dresses and have golden wings. She's cut them out of religious pictures, but hasn't used enough glue to make them stick to the page properly. I open the letter. I can just read it in the fading light. The writing is big, the lines aren't straight and Mum's spelling isn't good either. She had to leave school early to help support her family. It's just the usual stuff — Auntie Val's rheumatism is worse, Mr Dingley next door has had a stroke, Fred Knights has come back from the war with three fingers missing and a nasty scar on his face. I'm sorry to hear that Billy has left school and is working in a tinned fruit factory. Then at the end there's one sentence;

'Oh, I neerly forgot, Fred just got engagd to Sally Tucker and there weding will be in September.'

I feel like I've been hit by one of the shells, knocked sideways, concussed. I stare at the letter, watching the words fade into the darkness. It's quieter. The shells have died down a bit. Either that or I'm getting used to them.

I turn over the page and I can just read the Bible verse Mum's written on the back.

Behold, I give unto you power to tread on serpents and scorpions, and over all the power of the enemy: and nothing shall by any means hurt you.

Luke 10:19

When I left home, Mum just wanted me to keep my head down, but since she joined the Lady Mayoress's

Patriotic League, she's gradually changed her tune. Now she thinks we must be victorious and defeat the evil Huns at all costs.

I can see the shapes of men running. At first I think it's Germans. They're attacking. But then I realise it's our blokes. One of them dives down into the grass next to my shell hole. He's with the 58th, the battalion that was in reserve.

'New attack,' he says, out of breath. 'Us and the Tommies on the Sugar Loaf.'

He gets up and runs off.

The one soldier in the shell hole who is still conscious looks at me. He doesn't speak but I can tell from his eyes that he thinks I am scum. I look at Mum's paper angels. I fold up the letter and put it back in my pocket.

I don't have to be a coward. I can join this new push. I can show Sally that I am as brave as Fred Knights.

I get up and reach for my rifle, fix my bayonet. I climb out of the shell hole and run forward with the men of the 58th. I can't make out the Sugar Loaf in the dark, but I can see the red dots of the machine-gun fire. It's close. I aim my rifle, but it won't fire. It must have gotten wet in the shell hole. I keep running anyway. The enemy machine-gun fire is ferocious, like a horizontal hailstorm. Men are falling all around me. Then I can see it — a dark mound spitting out red from its black eyes like a crouching monster. The Sugar Loaf. The bullets are like a swarm of hornets flying fast and arrow-straight. One stings me in the leg, but I keep running. Another hornet stings me in the arm. I'm past the Sugar Loaf. I will make it to the German trenches where I can kill enemy soldiers with my bayonet. I will be a hero. I'll go home with medals.

I feel a sting in my back. My legs stop moving and I find myself face down in the dirt. It's cold. I'm cold. I slowly roll over and warm my hands in the blood that is coming through my jacket. I can see the first stars through the smoke. I can hear someone shouting orders in German. I'm close to the enemy trenches. I'll catch my breath and then I'll get up again and I'll kill the serpents and scorpions with my bayonet. I'll be a hero.

The surviving British are now all back in their own trenches. Only the Australian 15th Brigade takes part in the attack on the Sugar Loaf — half a battalion against the entire line of Germans. The German machine gunners at the Sugar Loaf turn all their firepower on the Australians. They are annihilated. None of them reaches the German lines. Major Hutchinson and most of the 15th Brigade soldiers now lie in no-man's-land, dead or wounded.

'Few more gallant episodes than this dashing, hopeless assault exist in the annals of any army in the war... The attack melted into nothingness — passed in a few quivering moments from the realm of man's high endeavour to the record of his deathless failures.'

Captain A D Ellis, 29th Battalion, 8th Brigade

At 9.25 p.m., Brigadier General Elliott receives notification from General Haking that the 9 p.m. attack has been cancelled.

9.30 p.m.

In growing darkness, the remains of four Australian battalions are furiously digging in behind enemy lines under constant artillery fire, but they have few officers to organise them. A new front line in enemy territory has only been established on the left and centre of the battlefront, and that is disconnected, the soldiers spread thinly. Somehow men have managed to haul a few machine guns across no-man's-land to the new front line.

'...there were men there with legs off, and arms hanging by a skin, and men sightless, with half their face gone, with bowels exposed, and every kind of unmentionable wounds...'
Lieutenant Hugh Knyvett, 59th Battalion, 15th Brigade

But the Germans have regrouped. They have brought in their own reserves. While the Australians stumble around in the dark in unfamiliar territory, the Germans have intimate knowledge of their own trench system as well as every feature of the land — every ditch and every clump of grass.

The Germans begin a counterattack. Soldiers of the 8th Brigade on the far left of the battlefront come under heavy fire.

Carrying parties arrive with ammunition and other supplies, and when they see how thinly manned the new front line is, many of them decide to stay and help their comrades instead of returning for more supplies.

10 p.m.

Information from the battlefield comes back in fragments — tied to a pigeon's leg, scribbled on a page torn from a New Testament, babbled by the wounded. General Haking still believes that some of the British troops on the right have taken their section of the German line. He orders another attack on the Sugar Loaf by the British Sixty-first Division, this time before dawn, under cover of darkness.

As Brigadier General Elliott is coming to terms with the fact that he has ordered his men to make a suicidal attack, he receives a request from Major General McCay to support Haking's newly planned attack on the Sugar Loaf. Elliott cannot refuse.

'And the sandbags were splashed with red, and red were the fire steps, the duckboards, the bays. And the stench of stagnant pools of blood of heroes is in our nostrils even now.'

Private W H Downing, 57th Battalion, 15th Brigade

Exploding shells have piled up earth, which has blocked the River Laies and the water has diverted to the ditches where the Australian soldiers are trying to construct the new front line. The water level in the new trench is rising. Added to the risks for the men is the chance of drowning if they are wounded and become unconscious. It also makes it hard to keep their rifles dry.

On the left, the 8th Brigade manages to repel the German counterattack. But on the right, the 14th Brigade is struggling. Major General McCay did not give any orders for the soldiers to **garrison** the old German line, so the Australian soldiers have left most of this trench undefended.

Captain Arblaster's battalion believes that the 15th Brigade is somewhere to the right of them, but as flares briefly light up the old German trenches to the right, the Australian soldiers are shocked to see the spiked helmets of German soldiers moving along them. Arblaster sends out bombing parties to crawl over open ground and take up positions in shell holes, from where they hurl grenades at the approaching enemy. They fight hard, but the Australians are eventually forced back.

11 p.m.

The British are all safely back in their trenches, but the Australians are not ordered to withdraw. Major General McCay informs his brigade commanders that they must take and hold all of their original objectives.

Ammunition is in short supply. There are not enough shovels and sandbags to create a strong defensive position. The 8th and the 14th Brigades hold their positions, but, even though they have received reinforcements, they don't have enough men to close the gap between them.

Towards midnight, against all odds, engineers have managed to dig a communication trench across no-man's-land to the 14th Brigade's position. Now men can travel back and forth and much needed ammunition and equipment arrives. The 8th Brigade, however, is still short of supplies and men crawl around collecting the guns and ammunition of the dead.

The Germans begin a second counterattack on the Australians who are trying to dig the new front line, attacking them from left and right.

Midnight

Until now, Brigadier General Elliott has clung to the hope that one of his battalions has made it to the German trenches. At half past midnight, this last hope is shattered. He receives a message from the battlefield informing him that none of the 15th Brigade ever reached the German front line. All of his men are in no-man's-land — either dead or wounded. Those who are able to are crawling back to their trenches. The attack by Elliott's brigade has been a complete failure.

When he hears this news, Major General McCay, heartless as ever, informs General Haking that the 15th Brigade will be 'of no further use in the attack'.

The battle is over for the 15th Brigade.

1 a.m.

The 8th and the 14th Brigades are still fighting to hold the new front line, but constant fire from German troops breaks up the tentative line even more.

Most of the reserves have been committed and the carrying parties have been absorbed into the attacking battalions.

AWM E04030

No-man's-land taken from the north-east corner of the Sugar Loaf, November 1916.

2 a.m.

On the right flank of the battlefront, it is only now that Lieutenant Colonel Cass, one of the 14th Brigade's battalion commanders, finally realises that the 15th Brigade is not on his right. German soldiers advance further along their old front line enabling them to shoot at the 14th Brigade from behind. The brigade is split into isolated groups.

On the left flank, a renewed German artillery assault commences from the direction of Delangré Farm.

3 a.m.

The Germans have recaptured their front line trench behind the 14th Brigade. Captain Arblaster and his men are cut off and almost out of ammunition. The young officer decides that the only thing left for his battalion to do is retreat. But to do that they must fight their way back through the Germans. He orders his men to turn around and charge the Germans in the old enemy front line. Arblaster is wounded and taken prisoner by the Germans.

Captain Charles Arbalaster was treated at a German POW hospital but died of his wounds on 24 July 1916, aged 21. This is a next-of-kin plaque issued to his father in 1922.

AWM REL06480

German soldiers reoccupy the Kastenweg and advance along their old front line from the left. The soldiers of the 8th Brigade on the left flank find themselves almost surrounded by the enemy, shot at from three sides. One battalion has lost its commander and they also decide that their only option is to retreat. They turn around and charge back through the Germans. Many are shot. Only a few survive to cross no-man's-land and return to their own trenches.

4 a.m.

Dawn is breaking. The pre-dawn assault of the British Sixty-first Division against the Sugar Loaf has not taken place.

5 a.m.

The soldiers of Lieutenant Colonel Toll's 8th Brigade battalion have seen their comrades retreat and they begin breaking back across no-man's-land. Lieutenant Colonel Toll cannot control them, and has no choice but to retreat himself.

There is a conference at General Haking's headquarters. While he is deciding what to do next, he hears the news that the 8th and the 14th have failed, and the second English assault never took place.

He orders that the battle be abandoned.

6 a.m.

Lieutenant Colonel Cass and the remainder of the 14th Brigade are the only Allied soldiers left on the battlefield. A runner is sent with the order to withdraw, but he is shot before he reaches the 14th's position. Another runner is sent, and another. They are both killed.

'…Wounded were crawling about here and there but mainly lying as near the parapet as possible waiting for stretcher bearers who never seemed to come, a lot of them hardly uttering a sound although they had been badly hit. One passed…hands, arms, legs, quite detached from their bodies. One chap had his head cut clean off by a shell.'

Private Leslie Martin, 8th Brigade machine gunner

7 a.m.

Runner after runner is sent out with the message to withdraw; they are all killed. Finally, the eighth runner makes it to Lieutenant Colonel Cass. It has taken almost two hours for the message to get through. Allied artillery fire shields the sad remains of the 14th Brigade as they move back to a segment of the old German line which is still unoccupied. The Germans are closing in on either side.

8 a.m.

Fifty men stay behind to cover the last of the 14th Brigade as they retreat along the communication trench that has been dug across no-man's-land.

Some defy the order to retreat, and shoot until they run out of ammunition and are forced to surrender. Men die within sight of their original trenches in the last minutes of the battle. The communications trench is so full of the dead and wounded, that some men climb out to make their retreat, but German snipers are waiting to pick them off.

'No English came into the trenches of the Regiment that day except as prisoners.'
Captain Friedrich Wiedermann, 16th Bavarian Reserve Infantry Regiment

9 a.m.

The last few men of the 14th Brigade stagger back and find the Australian front line trenches packed with wounded men. The battle is over. Nothing has been gained.

Chapter 6
Defeat

20 July 1916, Fleurbaix Sector, Western Front, France
Sergeant Frank Crawford,
60th Battalion, 15th Brigade

What a sad sight. Yesterday my battalion was a thousand strong. A thousand living, breathing, joking, smiling soldiers. Now there is just this handful of grim, grey-faced men, looking years older than they did yesterday. These are the survivors. The 60th Battalion has been almost wiped out in its very first engagement.

As there are so few officers left, I'm in charge of the roll call. I can't bring myself to call out all the names and listen to the silence, so I get the survivors to call out their names and I tick them off. Just 60 men and four officers. I can't believe it. We've lost more than 750 men. God help us if the Germans decide to attack today. There's only half a battalion of exhausted men in the front line.

McAlister wasn't at roll call.

I go over to a corporal from my company.

'Did you see McAlister out there?'

He shakes his head.

He's not at the dressing station either.

I just want to lie down and sleep, but the sun's burnt off the mist and you can see the dead and wounded lying out in no-man's-land. And now that the guns have finally stopped, you can hear wounded men calling out. It's awful. Orders are to wait until it's dark to attempt to rescue them, but it's going to get hot out there. Those that aren't already dead soon will be. And young McAlister might be one of them.

The 60th Battalion survivors are dead on their feet, but I say, 'I need some volunteers.'

They look at me in disbelief, wondering what on earth I want them to do. Dig out the ruined trenches? Rebuild the parapets?

'Officially, we're not supposed to go out and bring in any wounded, not until nightfall,' I say. 'But nobody said we couldn't go out and give 'em water.'

Six men volunteer. They look like they've suddenly found a store of energy. Perhaps they feel the same as me. Guilty. Did I do everything I could? Did I try hard enough? How come I'm still alive when so many are dead?

We fill up as many water **canteens** *as we can. Some of the boys take off their jackets and won't even put on helmets. They think there's less likelihood of the Germans shooting at them if they see them in their shirts with no weapons. It's a risk. I don't want any more of these lads to die, but I can't stand here listening to those cries for help.*

We go out, keeping to a low crouching run like monkeys. No one shoots at us, but we distribute the water canteens on our hands and knees, not taking any chances. The wounded are in a terrible state. It's warm and the flies are troubling them something shocking. I was at Gallipoli, but I've never seen wounds like these, and so many.

I hand a water canteen to one man. He lifts his hand an inch or two and dies before my eyes. There's another bloke in the same shell hole. His legs are both broken, bones shattered by machine-gun fire.

'I'll come back for you when it's dark,' I tell him.

'Don't think I'll still be here then.'

I look at him. He's probably right. 'It's dangerous in the daylight,' I say. 'But I'm game if you are.'

He nods. He's not a heavy bloke, but it's hard for me to lift him onto my back. I have to lie flat in the mud and blood. He rolls over and it's agony for him but he hangs on to my neck and I manage to get him onto my back. I crawl back to our trenches. A couple of the other boys are helping the wounded too. It has done them in though. They can't do it again. No one found McAlister.

A rumour has come down the line that someone up in the 8th Brigade is organising a truce to collect wounded. I have to go out again. I've got to find McAlister. I have this vague hope he might still be alive out there. It's stupid, I know, but I've kept an eye on him since Marseilles. He's obviously under-age; hasn't even started shaving yet.

I get a Red Cross armband from one of the stretcher bearers. I go out into no-man's-land again, though it's the last place on earth I want to be. I distribute more water. I bind up some wounds.

I must have a death wish. I'm almost at the German trench. The dreaded Sugar Loaf is over to my right.

Then I see him. McAlister. Lying in the churned up earth.

I crawl over to him. His uniform is soaked with blood. He's got something clutched in his hand. A photo I think. His eyes have the glazed look of the dead.

I'm just about to get his identification tag when I hear someone cock a rifle. I freeze. Close my eyes. Hold my breath. Wonder if I should pray. Nothing happens. I open my eyes. There's a German standing over me, pointing his rifle at me, his finger on the trigger. He looks as tired as I feel. He glances at McAlister.

'Junge,' *he says.*

I think that's German for 'young'. *I nod.*

The German points his rifle at my heart. 'Ein, zwei…'

He's counting. He's giving me time to get away.

'Drei, vier...'

I start running. I don't know whether he's counting to a hundred or to ten. The back of my neck is prickling. A couple of minutes ago I could hardly put one foot in front of the other, now I'm running faster than I ever have in my life.

IN THE GREY light of a new day, the awful sights of defeat were revealed. The Australian front line trenches, badly damaged by German artillery fire, were full of the dead and the dying. Many of the wounded had been lying there since the German artillery attacks before the battle started.

Hundreds of bodies lay out in no-man's-land. The trenches dug across no-man's-land during the night for the purpose of supplying the new front line, were now clogged with wounded men. Others were crawling back to their lines.

Aftermath

The German artillery was still firing. The entire Australian front line was held by just three half-battalions. If the Germans had decided to counterattack at that point, they probably could have taken that section, but they didn't. The guns of both sides persisted until midday when, finally, they fell silent. The silence only emphasised the extent of the terrible defeat.

Brigadier General Elliott made his way through the destroyed trenches, stepping

'There followed a stillness never again experienced by the Fifth Division in the front trenches. The sight of the wounded lying tortured and helpless in no-man's-land, within a stone's throw of safety but apparently without hope of it, made so strong an appeal that more than one Australian, taking his life in his hands, went out to tend them.'

Captain C E W Bean, Official Australian War Historian

over the bodies that were once his loyal soldiers. With tears streaming down his face, he consoled the wounded and exhausted survivors of the 15th Brigade, trying to convince them, and himself, that he had done all he could for them.

The Dreadful Tally

The battle was finally over. The remains of the battalions were back in the trenches where they had started. Not a centimetre of ground had been won. In fact, the position of the front line in the Fleurbaix sector stayed exactly the same for another two years.

As the remnants of the Australian battalions gathered for roll call on 20 July, the extent of their losses was shockingly obvious. More than 5,500 men were absent. In less than 24 hours, 1,700 men had died and another 200 would die from their wounds in the days after the battle. More than 3,000 were incapacitated by wounds and 470 had been taken prisoner by the enemy.

The British had lost 1,547 men — 519 dead, 977 wounded, 51 taken prisoner. It had been a devastating defeat. So many men had died, and no ground had been gained. The loss of officers was particularly high. It seems that the Germans snipers and machine gunners had specifically targetted officers, knowing that without leaders there would be confusion and a breakdown of command.

Australian Casualties at Fromelles

	Killed in action	Died of wounds	Prisoners of war	Wounded in action	Total
8th Infantry Brigade	477	51	166	1,086	1,780
14th Infantry Brigade	438	58	283	948	1,727
15th Infantry Brigade	726	98	5	904	1,733
Other units	60	9	16	208	293
Total	**1,701**	**216**	**470**	**3,146**	**5,533**

Night and Day

During that awful night, the infantry had not been the only ones working. The engineers had also been busy, digging trenches across no-man's-land to carry supplies to the new front line, but during the night, the purpose of the trenches changed. They became an escape route for retreating soldiers.

Stretcher bearers had risked their lives to bring in as many wounded as they could. Medical staff had attended to the wounded, but there were not enough of them to cope with the huge numbers of injured men. The aid posts were close to the front line, and medical officers had to examine their patients in the dark for fear that lights would attract German gunfire.

The medical staff worked through the night of the battle and all the following day, tending soldiers with horrific wounds — arms and legs blown off, faces ruined by gunfire. They also tended to those with no visible wounds, but with nerves shattered.

'We could not show a light and when we came to a wounded man we would ask him where he was hit and feel for his wound with hands covered with dried blood and mud. There was no time and no water to wash hands…'

Captain F W D Collier, Australian Army Medical Corps

A German World War I Red Cross poster.

Bringing in the Wounded

Many wounded men still lay out in no-man's-land and were calling for help. Private Miles, from the 8th Brigade, was one of those who braved the shell fire to help bring in the wounded. As he ducked from one shell hole to another, he got closer and closer to the German line, until he was so close he could hear a German calling to him. The German, an officer, spoke excellent English, and Private Miles defended his right to collect up the wounded without being fired upon. The German officer seemed to agree.

Since Miles had no authority to make such a decision, the German soldier allowed him to go back and find a superior who could authorise a truce, so that both sides could collect their dead and wounded from no-man's-land. Miles returned to the German front line with an officer, and the terms of the truce were agreed on, but permission was needed from a higher authority. A message was sent to Major General McCay.

There had been other similar truces earlier during the war, but the generals had banned them. They believed that such events made the enemy more human and were bad for the men's fighting spirit. McCay wasn't the sort of man to go against orders, so he refused to give permission. Both sides had used the negotiation time to rescue wounded soldiers, but most of the Australian wounded continued to lie dying in no-man's-land.

Endurance

But McCay was six kilometres away from the terrible scene of the battle, and the men in the trenches were not as hard-hearted as their commander. They could not ignore the plaintive cries of the wounded or the feeble hands raised in silent pleas for rescue. For the next three days, in daylight and under cover of darkness, Australian soldiers continued to bring in the wounded under German fire.

Some wounded soldiers lay in muddy shell holes with festering wounds for days, hoping for rescue. One man survived for more than a week, drinking the muddy water in the shell hole and eating rations taken from his dead comrades.

'We found the old no-man's-land simply full of our dead… the skulls and bones and torn uniforms were lying about everywhere.

Australian soldier visiting no-man's-land in November 1918

The dead had to be left where they were. More than two years later, when soldiers visited the site of the battle at the end of the war, they found the area still scattered with the remains of dead Australian soldiers.

The Germans were unimpressed by the way the Australians abandoned their dead. Perhaps if they had been the ones ordered to attack they would have understood, but it wasn't the Germans who had charged into no-man's-land to be slaughtered.

The furthest they had to go to collect their dead was just beyond their parapets.

POWs

Among the casualty figures were those soldiers taken prisoner by the Germans. Some of them died from their wounds in captivity. Those who could walk were marched through the town of Lille to humiliate them and show the French civilians that the Germans had triumphed. They were then transported to one of the many prisoner of war camps in Germany where they were held for two years and made to work in factories and mines.

During World War I, 2.5 million Allied soldiers were captured by the Germans. The total number of soldiers taken prisoner by all armies was more than 7 million.

Cover up

Letters from Australian and British soldiers serving in France were censored by the army. Officers read their letters before they were sent home and blacked out any specific information about military operations. Newspaper articles were also censored. This was because the British commanders didn't want the enemy to discover their plans, but censorship served another purpose. It allowed the military to conceal any bad news that might lower the morale of the civilians at home. The army didn't want the people's enthusiasm for the war to wane. Defeats such as that at Fromelles needed to be kept secret.

The English newspaper *The Times* reported that the battle had been a complete success. Instead of saying the Allies had been forced to retreat from the German trenches, the article said they 'stayed there for a while and then came away', making it sound like they had chosen to retreat.

An official communiqué was issued by the British Army the day after the battle. It referred to the battle as 'some important raids'. It reported that German prisoners had been taken, but made no mention of the Allied losses.

'Yesterday evening, south of Armentières, we carried out some important raids on a front of two miles in which Australian troops took part. About 140 German prisoners were captured.'

Official British Communiqué, 20 July 1916

The official German communiqué didn't beat about the bush. It listed estimates of the number of enemy dead. In Australia, it wasn't until after the war that the full extent of the losses became known.

What's in a Name?

The British newspapers didn't use the word 'battle' to refer to the Allied attack on 19 July. They called it 'a lively skirmish' and 'a big raid'. Captain Bean wrote an article that appeared in the *Sydney Morning Herald* and the Melbourne *Argus* newspapers on 24 July. He knew that the complete truth would not get past the censors. He followed the official story, emphasising the limited success and the taking of prisoners, but he managed to work elements of the truth into his article. He called the engagement 'an attack'. He told of the retreat of those who had made it across to German territory. In his final sentence, he said the losses were 'severe'. It was as close to the truth as he was permitted to get.

'The English attack in the region of Fromelles on Wednesday was carried out… by two strong divisions. The brave Bavarian Division, against whose front the attack was made, counted on the ground in front of them more than 2000 enemy corpses.'
Official German Communiqué, 21 July 1916

When Bean came to write his massive history of Australia's part in World War I, he didn't hesitate to refer to the events as the Battle of Fromelles. He devoted two chapters and 119 pages to those 24 hours of disaster. The official British history account was a brief 16 pages, and referred to it as a 'subsidiary attack'.

What upset Australian soldiers who had fought

'Britain bleeds from thousands of wounds as never before during the empire's existence. When the small results and enormous losses become known the British cries of victory will soon be silenced...'

Berliner, 24 July 1916

at Fromelles was that this playing down of the severity of the battle belittled their efforts through that awful night. Their mates who had died were not properly honoured for their sacrifice.

Broken

The newly established Fifth Division had been decimated. Just four months after its formation, it had to rebuild its ranks and its morale. The 15th Brigade in particular, which had only four officers left, took a long time to rebuild. It wasn't until September that the Fifth had the numbers and the confidence to take part in raids on the Germans again.

As the Australian soldiers saw it, the British troops had let them down. They had not done their job. Any trust or respect that they had for the British Army disappeared.

'...the loss was not in numbers only, for our very finest officers, NCOs and men, many of them Gallipoli veterans, perished there. And what did it accomplish?'

Brigadier General Harold Elliott, *The Duckboard*, 1 September 1930

Victims

Haig and Haking, who devised the disastrous battle, received no censure for its failure, but some of the commanders below

After the war it took Charles Bean 23 years to compile The Official History of Australia in the War 1914–1918 *using army records and the 226 notebooks he had filled during his four years at the battlefront. The history consists of 12 volumes containing almost 4 million words.*

them were punished. Major General McCay discovered Colonel Pope, commander of the 14th Brigade, asleep at 3 p.m. the day after the battle. He couldn't wake him. He decided that Pope was drunk, sacked him and sent him back to Australia. Two British Generals were also sacked.

Haig and Haking both continued to serve until the end of the war and were much honoured.

Of the six commanders who led the attacking battalions, not one of them made it through the battle unscathed. Lieutenant Colonel Toll was wounded in the head before the battle commenced, but survived the battle and the war. Major McCrae and Lieutenant Colonel Norris were killed in the first half hour. Norris had never seen action before. Captain Arblaster, the young officer who took over from Norris, was wounded, taken prisoner and died of his wounds five days later.

Unsuitable for Command

The 'wounds' of the other three battalion commanders were never acknowledged. They all suffered from shell shock, a mental condition that was little understood in 1916.

Lieutenant Colonel Harris, from the 15th Brigade, is recorded as being 'disabled' early in the battle. His commission was terminated and he was sent back to Australia. Lieutenant Colonel Coghill, the 8th Brigade battalion commander who was trying to set up the new front line, commanded his men well and Captain Bean recorded several heroic acts during the battle. Then around midnight, he disappeared from Bean's account, and someone else took charge of his battalion. Coghill relinquished his command a week later. He was said to be 'unsuitable' as an officer. McCay reported that he was 'unequal to the nerve-strain of command'.

Lieutenant Colonel Cass of the 14th Brigade commanded his battalion effectively throughout the battle, and was one of the last to leave the battlefield. He didn't succumb to shell shock till the following day, when the loss of his men troubled his mind. 'This is not war. They have murdered my boys!' he said, and it wasn't the Germans he was calling murderers. Cass was invalided to England a few days later. He relinquished his command and was given a desk job.

'One of our lieutenants got shell shock, and he literally cried like a child. Some that I saw carried down out of the firing line were struggling and calling for their mothers, while others were blabbering sentences one could not make out. For one to get shell shock it is worse than a wound…a wound will heal…'

Private Leslie Martin, 8th Brigade machine gunner

Brigadier General Elliott, a big bull of a man, never really got over Fromelles. One historian has said it 'seared his soul'. After the war, Elliott gave lectures about the battle, cataloguing the 'blunders' made by the commanders.

He was still writing articles about Fromelles in 1930. In 1933, he committed suicide.

Men who were afflicted with shell shock were thought to be weak and 'nervous'. They are not listed among the heroes. Losing your life in war is honourable; losing your sanity is not.

In World War I, shell shock was considered to be something that happened to a person if a shell exploded very close to them, like a serious ***concussion****. Nowadays it is known to be a nervous disorder brought about by the stress of experiencing the horrors of warfare.*

Chapter 7
What Went Wrong?

20 July 1916, Steenbecque, France
Sergeant Frank Crawford,
A Company, 60th Battalion, 15th Brigade

Of all the things I thought I might be doing in the army when I joined up, this isn't one of them. Typing. Some of the officers know how to type properly, but I can only do it with two fingers. I have to write condolence letters to the families of the battalion's dead.

This typewriter has seen better days, and the ribbon is nearly worn out. The purple letters on the page are faint, and all the Os type out of line like they're trying to jump off the page. The paper's got mud splatters on it too. There are so many letters to write, it's going to take me a long time. Brigadier General Elliott's doing all the officers and Lieutenant Ellwood's taken on a heap, even though he's wounded. The rest fall to me.

I'm back in the barn where we're billetted. It's very quiet. Before the battle we hardly had room to move. Now we've got more room than we want. I've had a bath, put on a clean shirt and socks, and had a hot meal. I've slept for a few hours, but something has been playing on my mind. I kept dreaming of McAlister lying out there. Him in particular I feel responsible for. If only I'd let him go **AWOL**. *He'd be in prison, but he'd be breathing still. I had this idea that he'd be marked for life if he deserted. I didn't want his mother to be ashamed of him. So he did the honourable thing, and what good did it do him?*

I should have let him go.

I can't go back and get his body, I've got all these letters to type. Some of the lads have gone out, but they won't go that close to the German line. I was lucky. That German was still in shock, I reckon, seeing all those bodies lying out in no-man's-land. Now they'll have had time to gather their own dead, and they won't be so merciful.

McAlister never spoke about his father. There's a brother, I think, and his mum had to go out to work to support them. I can't send MacAlister's identity tag, but I've been through his haversack. There's not much there, but it'll be something to remember him by — a scarf, his wallet, a camel carved out of wood that he bought in Egypt. I've put them in a sandbag and sent them to Brigade Headquarters. Eventually they'll find their way to his mother.

I wish I could tell her that her son had a proper, respectful funeral and there's a nice headstone to commemorate him, but the truth is he's lying out in no-man's-land and he'll probably just rot there. I feel bad, but there's nothing I can do. Except type this letter.

Dear Mrs McAlister,

This is a very difficult letter for me to write, and it will cause you a great deal of pain and sorrow, for I regret to tell you that your son Private Walter McAlister was killed in action. It occurred last night about fifteen minutes past nine, in an operation against the enemy. For reasons of security, I am not able to give you any details, but I can tell you that he was most brave and died from a bullet wound in the chest, so close did he engage with the enemy. I saw his body myself. He still bore his pleasing features, and I shall always remember him as I knew him – cheerful, helpful and hopeful, a fine Australian soldier.

I write to offer you my deepest sympathy in your sorrow, which will be very great I know. I have lost many a good friend since 1914, and I know the bitter loss when one who is very dear is taken away. His personal belongings will be sent to you through the proper channels. As commander of A Company, I am in a position to know your son's worth. I got to know him on the journey from Egypt to France. He always did his duty well. If ever he was asked to do a job he did it thoroughly. He was a young man I had my eye on to recommend for promotion. His loss will be felt throughout the whole company. What your son has done for his country was the duty God wished him to do. I again express my deepest sympathy with you in your loss.

Yours in sorrow, Sgt F G Crawford,
A Company, 60th Battalion, 15th Brigade

THE ALLIES HAD more men and more artillery than the Germans, but they lost the Battle of Fromelles. The purpose of the battle was to make the Germans keep troops in the area. They were supposed to believe that there was a big Allied troop build-up opposite them. If the Germans had ever believed that there was a large contingent of Allies, after the battle they knew for certain there wasn't, as they found a copy of the order issued by General Haking on a prisoner of war. It spelt out that the attack had only ever been a feint.

Why the battle went so tragically wrong is a topic that is still debated almost a hundred years after the event.

Inexperienced

The artillery had been rushed into action and many of the gunners had no battle experience. The Allied artillery failed to destroy key enemy positions and to disable the enemies' artillery.

One of the main reasons for the defeat was the fact that the inexperienced artillery had not destroyed the Sugar Loaf in the pre-battle bombardment. This gun emplacement, with thick concrete walls, was a crucial target. Because of the way the Sugar Loaf projected out into no-man's-land, the German gunners could shoot at the Allied soldiers from the front as they first attacked, from the side as they passed by the Sugar Loaf, and then from behind, if they made it past. The result was that no

Allied soldiers on either side of the Sugar Loaf reached the enemy trenches.

Many of the infantry soldiers were inexperienced, and though the Australian Fifth Division and the British Sixty-first Division were fighting together, they were commanded separately. There was no combined infantry assault on the Sugar Loaf. The 15th Brigade was almost completely destroyed by the machine guns of the Sugar Loaf and the British 184th Brigade was ordered to retreat.

'...from the highest to the lowest we were all amateurs. The generals and staff of the Regular army, though professionals in name, had never been trained to fight Continental armies or deal with such masses of troops.'

Brigadier General J E Edmonds, Official British War Historian

Misinterpreted

The Allies had been ordered to take a German support trench behind the front line — but no such trench existed. Though all brigades had aerial photographs of the area, no one had interpreted them correctly. They had thought that there were second and third rows of trenches immediately behind the German front line, but in reality these were nothing but a series of waterlogged ditches. The German support lines were actually further back towards Aubers Ridge.

Major General McCay did not order his men to occupy the old German front line. Only Lieutenant Colonel Toll decided to take up his position in the abandoned German trenches. The other battalions left the German front line trench empty and tried to turn one of the ditches into a trench. There weren't enough Australian soldiers to construct a strongly defended, continuous trench; it was instead not much more than a series of unconnected, hastily dug holes.

On the right of the battlefront, no Allies made it to the German trenches. Once the German soldiers had regrouped, they were able to re-enter their own trenches and virtually surround the Australians who had crossed into enemy territory.

Announced

In trench warfare, whenever the infantry ventures out of their protective trenches to attack, they are exposed and very vulnerable. Enemy soldiers can fire on them without leaving the protection of their own trenches. That means taking the enemy by surprise is a crucial element in trench warfare. If the enemy is

'I presume there was some plan at the back of the attack but it is difficult to know what it was. One can only say — it was an Order. I trust those who gave the order may be made to realise their responsibility…'

Brigadier General Elliott,
24 July 1916

caught unawares, the attackers can cross no-man's-land without sustaining too many casualties.

After all the changes to General Haking's battle plan, the Battle of Fromelles had ended up being half a demonstration, and half an attack — what Brigadier General Elliott called 'a wretched, hybrid scheme'. A demonstration is a noisy exhibition of firepower intended to intimidate the enemy by a show of artillery strength. The infantry is not put at risk.

The Battle of Fromelles was announced long and loud by the seven-hour artillery attack. The Germans were on the alert, ready and waiting for the Allies to advance.

Visible

But perhaps the biggest flaw in the battle plan was that Allied commanders didn't realise that the Germans could see their preparations. The German artillery seemed to know exactly when and where the Allied troops were assembling before the battle. Australian soldiers were convinced that French spies in the villages where they were billetted had informed the Germans about their plans.

The truth was the Germans didn't need spies. Flanders is an extremely flat area. When the Germans dug in at the end of 1914, they occupied the only land that had any elevation — Aubers Ridge. Though the maximum height of the ridge is just 36 metres, that slight elevation was enough for them to observe the Allies' activities. They turned church spires into indestructible observation towers by reinforcing them with concrete. They also nailed rungs to tree trunks so that soldiers could climb up and watch through binoculars.

There were rumours that some French people were spies for the Germans. Stories spread that they ploughed their fields at certain angles, or left different coloured horses in particular fields as coded signs for observers in German aircraft.

During the days before the battle, German observers had noticed soldiers carrying battle supplies and creating ammunition dumps. They had watched the build-up of Allied troops in the front line, which could only mean that an attack was imminent. As Captain Bean wrote in his official history of the war, the Germans learnt of the impending attack 'by ordinary observation'.

Unfair

British soldiers were withdrawn to the trenches before 9 p.m., and then twice failed to attack throughout the night of the battle, leaving the Australians out on the battlefield unsupported. The official excuse for this failure was that the troops were being bombarded and the trenches blocked with wounded. General Haking didn't order any Australian troops to withdraw until the early hours of the next day, when some British soldiers were already back in their billets asleep.

Australian soldiers did not like being commanded by the British officers for whom they had so little respect. General Haking, in particular, has been blamed for the failure. Officers as well as ordinary soldiers thought that he was untrustworthy and a bully. Before the war he had been a lecturer at the Army Staff College and he had written a book on army training. He was a man who believed that the only way to win a war was by attacking. This method had worked in earlier wars when battles had involved a charge, but with trench warfare, it meant the certain slaughter of the attacking troops. General Haking had attempted similar attacks before, one in the same place just a few months earlier. They had all ended in defeat and terrible loss of life. As a result, Haking became known as 'the Butcher'.

Indecisive

From beginning to end, the Battle of Fromelles was marked by the indecisiveness of its commanders. Before the battle, the plan of attack was altered several times, the date changed, the number of divisions involved was revised. During the battle a second assault was ordered for 9 p.m., then rescheduled at the last minute, and finally cancelled altogether.

General Haking never learned from his mistakes and he took no responsibility for the failure of the Battle of Fromelles. He blamed it on the unfortunate men who he had sent to their death. He said that the artillery was inexperienced; the Australian infantry, though brave, had not had enough training; and the British soldiers lacked 'offensive spirit'. In fact, he blamed everyone but himself. He claimed that two well-trained divisions would have easily taken the German positions. In a final callous insult to the men who had fought at Fromelles, he claimed that the attack had 'done both divisions a great deal of good'. How a loss of almost half their comrades could do the men any good, is impossible to understand.

'The Australian infantry attacked in the most gallant manner and gained the enemy's position, but they were not sufficiently trained to consolidate the ground gained.'

Lieutenant General Haking, General Officer Commanding XI Corps, Official Report

Surviving soldiers and the Australian war historian Charles Bean did not agree with Haking. Modern war historians are also highly critical of his tactics.

Most Detested

Not all unpopular officers were British. Major General McCay was Australian, but he managed to inspire dislike in both officers superior to him and the men serving under him. His failure to order the garrisoning of the German front line was a major mistake. The men under his command had not forgotten the disastrous desert march back in Egypt, and his refusal to allow a truce to rescue the wounded was, for them, unforgivable. They despised him.

'The reasons for this failure seem to have been loose thinking and somewhat reckless decision-making on the part of the higher staff.'
Captain C E W Bean, Official Australian War Historian

Before the war, McCay had been a successful politician. He had been a strong advocate of women's right to vote, and was opposed to conscription. He had been wounded at Gallipoli. Yet it was his record on the Western Front that he was remembered for, and his unpopularity continued until his death. Those who write about the recently dead usually manage to find something good to say about the deceased, but that wasn't the case with McCay. When he died in 1930, his obituary remembered him as 'about the most detested man in the AIF'.

In the Dark

There was an almost total failure of communications in the battle. Although this was not uncommon during World War I, it was particularly bad at Fromelles. The latest technology — the telephone — was used for communication, but it was reliant on signallers laying metres and metres of wires from the front line trenches across no-man's-land to the new positions on the other side. It is not surprising that many of these wires were destroyed by shell fire, leaving the officers in the field out of communication with their headquarters.

'The English Enterprise against Fromelles has caused headshaking everywhere amongst ourselves as well as in neutral countries and perhaps even among the French and English themselves, for no-one could imagine what the intentions of the English really were.'

North German Gazette, 3 August 1916

Officers were forced to rely on 'runners' to send messages back and forth. This was an extremely dangerous job and many runners were killed before reaching their destination. In modern times it seems unbelievable that carrier pigeons were used to send messages from the battlefield. The small and fragile birds didn't always survive but, when they did, they could fly from the battlefield above the smoke and shells at a speed of up to 80 kilometres per hour to reach the lofts behind the lines in a few minutes. It was, however, a one-way communication. Homing pigeons will only fly back to their coops. They could not be sent out into the battlefield.

Commanding officers, kilometres behind the front line, didn't have accurate information about what was happening on the battlefield. Those in the midst of the battle were unaware of changes to orders, the position of the British division, the location of the other Australian brigades, or even the condition of their own men.

During the daylight hours, smoke made it difficult to see what was happening, and when night fell those in the field were literally in the dark. It is easy to understand how messages went astray on the battlefield, but delays in sending crucial orders from one command post to another behind the lines (such as the order sent to Brigadier General Elliott to cancel the proposed 9 p.m. attack) can not be blamed on battlefield conditions. Sometimes it seems staff were just incompetent.

Military pigeons were housed behind the battle lines in 'lofts' made from converted London buses.

AWM H09552

Chapter 8
Tommies, Frogs and Fritz

22 July 1916, Aubers-Fromelles Sector,
Western Front, France
Private Kretschmer,
3rd Battalion, 16th Bavarian Reserve Infantry Regiment

'The bodies of the enemy in front of the trench are a hazard to health.'

That is what the Kommandeur said. So we have to collect them and bury them. To be safe, we waited until it was dark. There are many bodies. Very many. We used stretchers which made it easier to carry them, but it was a terrible task. We had to load them onto a rail wagon.

The bodies have been transported back behind the lines. Now we have to bury them. They are starting to smell.

'Each body must be carefully searched,' the Kommandeur says. 'You must search every pocket. Take off identity discs, watches.'

I do not want to get so close to the bodies. It was bad enough lifting them off the stretchers and onto the wagons. That was enough. They should have got others to do this job.

'We want to learn all we can about these soldiers — which brigades they were with, which battalions. Perhaps the officers have orders in their pockets. Be vigilant. This information will help us defeat our enemies.'

I have searched ten English soldiers. Actually, they are not English. I did not recognise their badges, which have a sun, either rising or setting, but an officer told me that they are the insignia of Australian soldiers. Australia is a country far, far away. I do not understand why they have come across the world to fight with the English. Someone told me they were not forced to join their army, but volunteered.

It is a terrible job searching the pockets of dead men. And they are not only dead but horribly wounded, some torn apart.

The first I searched very thoroughly, looking in every pocket, opening his jacket to search in his shirt. I found a photograph of a wife and baby, a New Testament, also a white pebble. Perhaps it is a memento of his home, from his family's garden, or perhaps from a beach.

I unpinned his badges, ripped from his sleeve the cloth patch that identifies his battalion, took his identity discs and a cross from around his neck.

The Australians have very good boots, much better than ours. It is strictly against orders to take any personal items from the dead, but someone has decided that boots are equipment, so we are taking off their boots. I wonder if they will issue them to German soldiers? I don't like the idea of wearing a dead man's boots.

As the day wears on, I am not so thorough. Everyone has chosen the bodies with the least wounds first, and now the worst cases only are left. It is a warm day and the flies are persistent, covering the wounds. I turned over one man and his intestines slithered out onto the ground. It made me sick and I had to run into the bushes.

Now I am not hurrying, so I will have less bodies to search. And here is this soldier with his jacket stiff with dried blood. His face is very young. He is a boy, not a man. Younger than me, I think. In his pocket I find a letter. I cannot read English, so I don't know what it says. There is something else folded with the letter — paper angels, white with golden wings, or they would have been once, but now they are mostly stained with dark red. These angels did not protect him. I take his identity disc from his neck. He has something in his hand. I have to unclasp his stiff fingers to take it from him.

It is a photo of a pretty girl.

I take off one of his colour patches. It is a rectangle, half white, half red. I am still feeling sick, so I leave the other one. I go through his bag, but it contains only his food rations — two biscuits like rocks and a tin of meat — and his grenades. He did not throw them at us. I don't open his jacket to look in his shirt pockets. I leave him with some secrets to take to his grave.

At last the searching is finished. Others have dug pits and now we have to put in the bodies. We start off laying them carefully and neatly in rows, but there are so many — more than 200 — and it is exhausting work. We sprinkle the layers of bodies with chloride of lime. Towards the end we are not so careful. The bodies are thrown into the pit and are left however they land. Then at last we can cover them with the black mud.

HISTORICAL ACCOUNTS OF World War I written by British and Australian historians tend to focus on the exploits of their own troops. Because the Battle of Fromelles has been of great interest to Australians, most accounts focus on the Australian troops involved, with minimal mention of the others — allies or enemies — who took part in the battle.

Nicknames

Soldiers in World War I used slang to downplay the seriousness of fighting in deadly battles. An upcoming battle was referred to as a 'scrap', a 'show' or a 'stunt'. When a soldier spoke about the possibility of getting wounded, he referred to it as getting 'smacked' or 'cracked'. When a comrade was killed, he had 'gone west'.

A 'Blighty' was a wound, not life threatening, but bad enough for the soldier to be sent to a hospital in England. When the soldiers jumped over the sandbag parapets into a hail of deadly machine-gun fire, they said they were 'hopping the bags'.

Australians also had nicknames for the soldiers of different countries. They referred to themselves as Diggers, English soldiers were Tommies and the French were called Frogs. The enemy was called the Hun, the Bosche, but more often, Fritz.

The Enemy

Though the British officers in charge of the battle are blamed for the failure, the German Army were well organised, occupied higher ground, and managed their counterattacks well. Australia wasn't the only new nation flexing its muscles in this war. Thirty years before Federation in Australia, 39 separate states had united to form the German Empire. Young German soldiers were just as keen to fight for their nation as Australians were for theirs.

The soldiers in the opposite trenches during the Battle of Fromelles were from the Sixth Bavarian Reserve Division. This German division had been stationed in the trenches near Fromelles for more than a year. Whereas many of the Australian Fifth Division and the British Sixty-first Division were recruits, new to the Western Front, the Germans in the trenches opposite were experienced soldiers, very familiar with their own trench systems and the local area.

Five-star Trenches

The Germans had been establishing their front line for a year and a half, and they had done a very good job of it. Not only were they well placed to observe when the Allies were preparing for battle, they had also built excellent defences. German soldiers in the front line trench had concrete shelters where they could take refuge from artillery attacks. There were 75 of them along the battlefront at Fromelles, but despite the hours of Allied artillery fire, only 15 were destroyed.

Further back from the front lines, there were chambers six metres below ground (like the one that Lieutenant Colonel Cass set up in), which were equipped with comforts such as wallpaper, electric light and cigars. It wasn't only the officers who had comfortable facilities. There were dry underground rooms, protected by metres of packed earth which had bunks where ordinary soldiers could rest untroubled by heavy artillery fire. By contrast, if Allied soldiers had a chance for a few minutes sleep, the only shelter they had in the front line was in muddy holes dug roughly into the walls of the trenches. The only places to shelter from an enemy artillery attack were dugouts made of sandbags.

'I thank all my troops whose bravery and reliable cooperation made it possible to inflict severe defeat on the attackers, although we were outnumbered two to one, and together with the division I am awaiting possible storms in the future confident of succeeding.'

Lieutenant General Gustav Scanzoni von Lichtenfels, Commander, Sixth Bavarian Reserve Division

Strengths

The Allied commanders underestimated their enemy. The Germans were not fooled by the Allied barrage lifts. Despite the fact that the Allies waved their weapons above the parapets at the end of each barrage, the Germans did not believe an attack was about to occur and so they did not man their parapets. The machine gun bunkers like the Sugar Loaf were strongly built. The Allies had more big guns, but they were unable to disable the lethal German machine guns.

'Whenever someone was shot another took his place without being ordered, pressed his body against the breastworks, staring with burning eyes through smoke and dust of the fiery explosions to the enemy position in order not to miss the moment when the English would first commence their attack.'

History of the 16th Bavarian Reserve Infantry Regiment

Yet the battle was no walk-over for the Germans. Their casualties were 1,590, with 501 men dying, 943 wounded and 146 taken prisoner. But after the initial attack, they were able to regroup, and reinforcements were brought in. They took advantage of the fact that the Allies left the German front line trench undefended, and they reclaimed it.

They succeeded, and therefore the battle was a morale boost for the German soldiers, especially since they were fighting against a larger enemy force.

Corporal Hitler

The name of one German soldier who took part in the Battle of Fromelles was destined to become well-known around the world. That was Lance Corporal Adolf Hitler. He was a dispatch runner in the 16th Bavarian Reserve Infantry Regiment. It was his job to carry messages from the front line to regimental headquarters. In the Battle of Fromelles, his regiment was opposite the Australians.

'I was prepared to die at any time for my own kinsfolk and the Empire to which they really belonged.'

Adolf Hitler, *Mein Kampf*, 1925

During World War II, when Hitler had become president of Germany and commander of the German Army that had successfully invaded France, he returned to visit the Fromelles battlefield. He put up a plaque on the building where he had been billetted during the previous war.

The Allies

Historians are generally critical of the British officers who commanded the battle, but they do not think that the British soldiers were to blame for the defeat.

Like the Australians, many of the Tommies were inexperienced. The soldiers who made up the British Sixty-first Division consisted of 'Territorials' —

While his regiment was stationed near Fromelles, Hitler had a pet dog called Fucshl that had strayed over from the British lines. He also found time to do some water-colour paintings of the French villages.

Hitler in the German Army, 1914. Hitler is seated on the right.

soldiers who had signed up to act as a defensive force on British soil, not to fight overseas. However, due to the growing need for more British soldiers in Europe, these men had been sent to France. They were also new arrivals with little experience, having disembarked from England just six days before the battle.

Tough Job

The British 184th Brigade had the hardest job of the entire battle. They were the ones faced with attacking the Sugar Loaf and, like the Australians, they were badly hit in the trenches during the German pre-battle artillery attacks. The 183rd Brigade were so severely hit in the trenches that they had to call in their reserves before the battle had even started.

'By 5.30 we had lost nearly 100 men killed or wounded by shellfire...by 6 p.m. [the enemy] mowed down our advancing waves so that few even actually reached the German parapet.'

War Diary of 2/1st Buckinghamshire Regiment

The German trenches opposite the 182nd Brigade had been successfully destroyed and the wire cut, so these soldiers made it across no-man's-land with little loss. They took almost 100 German prisoners, but their success was short lived. A handful of German soldiers managed to set up three machine guns and drove the 182nd back.

Following Orders

The Tommies could only do what they were ordered to do, and their commanding officers made some bad decisions. When the battle began, the Australian soldiers 'hopped the bags'; they all jumped over the parapet in front of them at the same time. British soldiers were ordered to file into no-man's-land one at a time via breaks in the parapet called sally-ports. Once German observers had worked out where the sally-ports were, it was easy for their gunners to pick off the soldiers as they emerged.

'To have delivered battle at all, after hurried preparation, with troops of all arms handicapped by their lack of experience and training in offensive trench-warfare, betrayed a grave under-estimate of the enemy's powers of resistance.'

Brigadier General J E Edmonds, Official British War Historian

At around 8 p.m., the British soldiers were ordered to retreat to their trenches. Orders to make a fresh attack were cancelled. With hindsight, it might be considered that this made more sense than sending soldiers back into battle in the face of overwhelming defeat.

Where Were the French?

At Fromelles, the Australian and British soldiers were defending France against the Germans. Why were no French troops there defending their own country?

Reading British and Australian accounts of World War I, it's easy to form the impression that the French were hardly involved at all, as historians focus on the involvement of their own countrymen. Of course the French were fighting, but at different places.

In the opening stages of the war, the French Army fought against the invading Germans. As the German Army swept through Belgium and northern France to reach the outskirts of Paris, it was the French Army that was trying to hold them back. In the Battle of the Marne in September 1914, they succeeded, but at the cost of a quarter of a million French soldiers who were killed or wounded in just eight days.

At the time of the Battle of Fromelles, the French were defending three-quarters of the Western Front. They were fighting in two on-going battles — the Battle of the Somme, which lasted for four months, and the Battle of Verdun, which lasted for ten months. Millions of French civilians were living in German-occupied France, and many had been rounded up and were being used as forced labour.

More than 8 million French soldiers fought in World War I. Half of them ended up as casualties, and 1.3 million of them died.

A French World War I poster.

Ignoring the War

The French who were affected by the Battle of Fromelles were the people who lived in the area. Many had fled, but others were still trying to live their lives. Farmers worked their fields and children still attended school. The Allies took over villages, turning public buildings such as town halls into army headquarters and hospitals. Soldiers dug trenches through the farmers' wheat fields. Villagers had to billet soldiers in their homes or in their barns and stables.

'These were the days of long and casual bombardments... Stooping men and women watched the Australians pass, without ceasing their work... They tilled the fields on the edge of the flames, under the arching trajectory of shells.'

Private W H Downing, 57th Battalion, 15th Brigade

On the other side of the Western Front, the same things were happening, except those French civilians were being occupied by an invading enemy. The village of Fromelles was on the German side of the front line, less than two kilometres from the battlefield. Before the war, it had a population of about 1,000. It had around 200 houses, some farms and a 14th-century church. The Germans used the Church spire as an observation tower. For the Allied troops, Fromelles was a target. By the end of the war, the village was almost completely destroyed.

Australian soldiers having lunch by the roadside with French children.

WM EZ0110

Chapter 9
Pheasant Wood

23 October 2009, Melbourne, Australia
Tamora McAlister, Year 9,
Yarrabank High School

I wasn't interested in family history. No one in my family was, apart from Auntie Sue who I always thought was a bit weird. I didn't see the point of finding out about a lot of old dead people. But we got this school assignment, one of those that teachers love because students have to think up their own topic. We had to do a research project on an Australian in World War I.

My friend Jessica chose the Prime Minister of the day, Billy Hughes. Jack found out there was a famous

Collingwood player who fought in the war, so he's doing him.

I didn't have a clue. I asked Mum and Dad while we were eating dinner that night if they had any ideas. They weren't much help.

'I don't suppose one of my great grandfathers was in World War I?'

'My grandfather was,' Mum said, 'but he was English.'

Dad shook his head. 'My grandad was too young.'

I thought that was the end of it, but just as I was loading the dishwasher, Dad suddenly said, 'I think my Great Uncle Walter fought in World War I.'

'Who?' I'd never heard of Great Uncle Walter.

'He died in the war. He was my grandad's brother.'

The teacher had showed us where all the World War I soldiers' army records are online. So I looked him up.

I was disappointed. Uncle Walter was in the army for less than a year. He'd done some training in Egypt, arrived in France and was killed a few months later. He didn't do enough to fill a project.

A week later, I still hadn't come up with anyone to research. I'd printed out all 27 pages of Great Uncle Walter's records, but it was pretty boring so I'd only read the first few pages.

I was getting desperate, so I had another look at his records.

A lot of it was just the same information repeated,

but then I came to a page that was written in German. I thought he must have been a German spy or something, but in small writing on another page it said that his identity discs had been received from the German Red Cross. The Germans had found his body and buried it somewhere. There was also a note from his mother saying he was 18 and he had her permission to join the army. It was signed with a very dodgy-looking signature, like one of those notes Jack forges to say he's allowed to get out of school early.

I asked Dad about this.

'Walter fought in the Battle of Fromelles,' Dad said. 'His body was never found, that's all I know. I never heard anything about him being buried by the Germans.'

This was starting to sound more promising. I bet no one else has an uncle buried by the Germans!

I even rang Auntie Sue. She knew all about Walter. She emailed me his photo. He looks very young. She says his mother never got over his death and left his identity discs and a little wooden camel on his pillow in his bedroom for years. It's so sad. Auntie Sue has the discs and the camel now, and I'm going to take photos of them to put in my project.

I talked Dad into paying for Walter's birth certificate, which I could download from the internet.

Sure enough, he was only 17 when he joined up. He had forged his mother's signature. Poor Walter, he was only a couple of years older than me.

I googled the Battle of Fromelles. Turns out it was a complete disaster. We lost, and thousands of soldiers died, including Uncle Walter.

While I was online, I came across some recent news articles. They've found where the Germans buried Australian soldiers who died in the battle, hundreds of them. Now they are trying to identify them. It sounds creepy, but actually they are doing it with DNA. They want relatives to give a DNA sample so they can match it with samples taken from the dead soldiers.

Dad said he wasn't interested.

'You do it,' he said.

So I did. I was ready to stab my finger like diabetics have to, but, when the DNA kit arrived, all I had to do was wipe a cotton bud on the inside of my cheek and send it back.

The results came in the post today. My DNA matches one of the soldiers they've dug up. They've found Walter! It's a perfect ending for my project.

I think I understand why people get excited about family history now. Everybody is part of history, not just the famous people who get mentioned in history books.

Most of us don't have famous ancestors — they were just ordinary people going about their lives — but that doesn't mean they weren't taking part in important events

Like poor Walter. He took part in World War I.

He fought in a battle where many soldiers died unnecessarily. I don't know if he was a hero or not, but he died fighting for Australia. He's part of history.

Now he's part of another chapter of history — the discovery of the missing soldiers of Fromelles. And I guess I'm part of that chapter of history too.

AFTER THE WAR, the story of this particular battle faded from public memory until 2002, when a Melbourne high-school teacher brought the Battle of Fromelles back to public attention.

A Question

Lambis Englezos was born in Greece, but his family emigrated to Australia when he was one year old. His curiosity about World War I was aroused by Anzac Day commemorations in primary school. This schoolboy interest has grown into a lifelong passion.

Groups such as the Family and Friends of the First AIF are currently campaigning to have the Battle of Fromelles listed on the major war memorials in Australia that commemorate World War I.

The VC Corner Cemetery, just outside the village of Fromelles, is where the remains of 410 Australian soldiers who died in the Battle of Fromelles are buried. Their mangled bodies were collected from the battlefield after the war. None of these soldiers had headstones because their names were not known. Instead, a memorial wall was created that lists the names of 1,299 soldiers from the battle with no known grave. The names of the buried men were on that list, but no one knew which they were.

In 2002, while visiting the VC Corner Cemetery, Lambis sat down and did some arithmetic. Unidentified soldiers who died in the Battle of Fromelles are buried in a number of nearby war cemeteries. Lambis added them to those buried at VC Corner. According to his figures, there were still 163 men unaccounted for. Where were the remains of these missing soldiers?

Proof

Lambis began to dig around in the war records. Others who were infected by his enthusiasm joined the search. In the records of one of the missing soldiers, they found correspondence from the German Red Cross that mentioned burial pits at a place called Fasanenwald. In English, *Fasanenwald* means Pheasant Wood.

The name of this place also came up in the official history of one of the Bavarian regiments that took part in the battle, and again burial pits were mentioned. Lambis and his colleagues came up with the theory that the missing men had been buried by the Germans behind enemy lines. The evidence that really convinced Lambis was an aerial photograph taken a few months after the battle, which clearly showed eight rectangular pits alongside a wood. These features were not on a photograph taken before the battle. The local people called this wood Bois Faisan which is French for Pheasant Wood.

Further examination of the service records of the 1,299

soldiers listed on the VC Corner Cemetery came up with a list of 161 who had German Red Cross files, which stated their bodies had been collected and buried by the Germans. Now the missing soldiers had names. British soldiers were buried there as well. Altogether Lambis believed there could be as many as 400 bodies buried at Pheasant Wood.

Setback

Lambis and his colleagues were confident they had solved the puzzle and they approached the Australian Army for assistance in examining the Pheasant Wood site to prove their theory. A panel of experts was put together by the Army History Unit to listen to Lambis' argument, which they did in June 2005. The panel was not convinced. After the war, Graves Recovery Units (GRUs) had scoured the battlefields for the bodies of soldiers, identifying them where they could and burying them in the many war cemeteries that were being built around the battlefields in France and Belgium. The panel couldn't believe that the thorough GRUs had missed a mass grave of that size. They said the evidence wasn't strong enough to justify the expense of an archaeological excavation in France.

A search of the extensive German war archives took place. More evidence was uncovered, including a specific order from a German commander for graves to be dug behind Pheasant Wood for the burial of 400 enemy soldiers. While the panel agreed that the rectangles on the photographs looked like burial pits, they argued there was no proof that they were still full of bodies.

Pressure

As far as Lambis was concerned, the Australian Army had sent the soldiers under-prepared into an unwinnable battle. It had downplayed the importance of the engagement, refusing to even call it a battle. Now it seemed that the army would let them down again, by failing to do everything possible to locate their bodies. He believed that the dead wouldn't rest in peace until they were given a proper burial and commemoration.

'I felt like I knew the men we found. I had seen their photos as young men, as Australian soldiers. I had read the anguished letters of their mothers and fathers. These men were not at peace.'
Lambis Englezos, 2008

Interest in the search for the missing soldiers of Fromelles continued to grow, and it was mentioned in the Australian Parliament. A group of people called Recovering Overseas Australia's Missing Inc or ROAM, had also become involved in the campaign. They had found a sponsor willing to fund a private archeological dig at the Pheasant Wood site.

Now that it seemed possible that British soldiers were buried there as well, a British parliamentary war graves committee became interested. When the panel of experts met again, they conceded that there was a possibility that bodies were buried at Pheasant Wood, but that the evidence still wasn't convincing enough for a full-scale archeological dig to go ahead. Instead they recommended a preliminary archeological survey.

First Finds

A team from Glasgow University's Archeological Research Division (GUARD) was engaged for the job. In May 2008, they conducted geophysical tests that indicate if there are features buried beneath the earth. The tests confirmed that eight pits had been dug at the site. The next task was to prove whether the pits contained bodies or not. GUARD began an exploratory excavation.

Despite more than 90 years of ploughing and souvenir hunting, the fields of Flanders are still littered with remnants of the war such as buttons, shrapnel and shell casings. French farmers still unearth tonnes of live shells each year.

As they dug down, they unearthed two Australian rising-sun emblems. The battle had taken place a kilometre away, so they concluded that the badges must have come from the uniforms of men buried there. Finally, 1.2 metres down, they discovered bones. It was a grim discovery, but as they continued to dig, they found that they had unearthed a burial site containing many bodies.

It had taken six years, but Lambis Englezos had solved the puzzle. He had found the missing soldiers of Fromelles.

Exhumation

The project now had world-wide attention. A joint operation was organised which involved the cooperation of three governments — Australian, British and French. It was agreed that a full archeological dig would be undertaken to unearth the bodies. They would then try to identify them, and finally re-bury them in individual graves.

A team of 30 archaeological and forensic specialists began work at Pheasant Wood in May 2009. On their hands and knees using trowels, they carefully scraped away the muddy earth of Flanders, as they unearthed skeletal remains of the soldiers. Then they removed the bones and put any remnants of uniforms or personal belongings in plastic bags for individual examination.

They found the remains of 250 bodies.

Identification

Before they buried them, the Germans had searched the bodies for any identifying items such as identity discs, badges or personal letters. They did this for two reasons. Firstly they wanted to find out all the information they could about the enemy in the opposite trench — which country they were from, which division. Then, once they had learned what they could, each man's belongings were put in a bag, labelled and sent to the International Red Cross so that they could be returned to his family. This meant that there would be few clues buried with the bodies that could identify who they were.

'The misappropriation of even the most insignificant item of property from a body (either German or English) constitutes robbery of the dead and will be severely punished.'

Major General von Braun, 21st Bavarian Reserve Infantry Regiment, Order No. 5220, 21 July 1916

Searching the bodies of the dead and wounded would have been an unpleasant task, and the German soldiers given the task weren't as thorough as they might

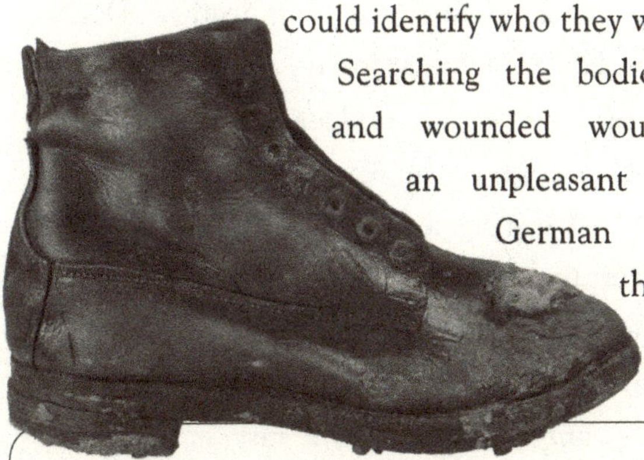

A boot still containing a sock, unearthed by archeologists at the mass war grave in Fromelles.

have been. The archaeological team found more than 6,000 artifacts buried with the men including items from their uniforms such as belt buckles, buttons and a boot. They also found personal items such as a ring, crucifixes, a compass, a lock of hair enclosed in a leather heart, and a return ticket from Fremantle to Perth.

The archeologists confirmed that 203 of the buried soldiers were Australian, while only three were British. It was not possible to determine the nationality of the other 44 soldiers.

DNA

Ninety-two years had passed since the soldiers were buried. In that time science had come up with a way to identify the long dead — DNA testing. DNA samples, in the form of a small piece of bone or an undecayed tooth, were taken from each of the recovered bodies.

In DNA testing, a person's identity can only be ascertained by comparing their DNA to another DNA sample. Police forensic officers compare DNA samples from a crime scene with a DNA sample taken from a suspect to see if they match. To identify the dead soldiers, the forensic team advertised for relatives of soldiers who had died at Fromelles to give DNA samples. This involved taking a swab from the inside of their cheek and sealing it in a test tube. To ensure that the DNA of the archaeologists did not contaminate the specimens collected, archaeologists had to wear protective suits and face masks. They also had to give samples of their own DNA to rule out contamination.

165,000 Commonwealth soldiers who fought on the Western Front are still missing.

By September 2010, 2,611 relatives had responded and given DNA samples, and 96 soldiers had been identified. All of those identified so far have been Australians. To allow more relatives to come forward, the DNA testing team will remain in operation until 2014.

Burial

With the world's attention on the village of Fromelles, things moved more speedily. It was decided that a new military cemetery would be built — the first one in Europe since World War II — to accommodate the dead of Fromelles. The Pheasant Wood site is not suitable for a cemetery as it is subject to flooding and difficult to access, and so a site was selected near the Fromelles Church, which had been rebuilt after the war.

The cemetery, which is called the Fromelles (Pheasant Wood) Military Cemetery, is hexagonal in shape and has a six-metre cross. The first soldier was buried there on 30 January 2010 with full military honours. Burials continued at intervals until the last soldier was buried at the cemetery's dedication ceremony on 19 July 2010, the 94th anniversary of the Battle of Fromelles. Each soldier has an individual grave and headstone with the inscription of the unknown soldier — Known unto God. If the identity of the soldier is discovered, the headstone is replaced with a new one that bears his name.

Statue

The Australian Memorial Park, less than two kilometres from the new Fromelles Military Cemetery, also commemorates those who fought in the Battle of Fromelles. It was created on the site of the German trenches that Australians briefly captured during the battle. In 1998, a statue was commissioned for the park. Sculptor Peter Corlett created

The primary school in the village of Fromelles is called L'école des Cobbers, in honour of the Australian soldiers who fought in France. It has two clocks — one showing the local time, the other Australian Eastern Standard Time. It also has a weathervane with a kangaroo on top.

The Cobbers statue, the Australian Memorial Park, France.

a bronze sculpture of Sergeant Simon Fraser of the Fifth Division rescuing a wounded comrade from no-man's-land. He called the statue 'Cobbers'.

Lambis Englezos wasn't content with a commemorative statue in France. He wanted one in Melbourne as well. It took him a number of years to find sponsors to pay for a new sculpture to be cast, but he succeeded. A twin of the Cobbers statue was unveiled in the gardens of the Melbourne Shrine of Remembrance on 19 July 2008.

'Your spirit will never be lost from our land and our hearts. We have been brothers until death, you have had your blood spilled for us and there is no bond stronger than that. From the bottom of our hearts, we express our eternal gratitude for your sacrifice.'
Guillaume Mooreel, present-day resident of Fromelles

The Battle of Fromelles is still officially considered to be part of the Battle of the Somme. There is no mention of Fromelles on any war memorial in Australia. Those who died there are listed under the Battle of the Somme.

POSTSCRIPT

BY THE END of World War I, the army's attitude to infantry soldiers had changed. They were no longer considered to be entirely dispensable. The deaths of thousands of men could not be casually dismissed as a necessary part of a battle. Technology came to the aid of the humble infantry man in the form of tanks and more accurate artillery.

In May 1918, Australians were finally permitted to command their own army — something that had been called for since the beginning of the war. When General John Monash became Commander of the Australian Corps, he had a different attitude to Haig and Haking.

> *'The true role of infantry is not to expend itself upon heroic physical effort, not to wither away under merciless machine-gun fire, not to impale itself on hostile bayonets, but on the contrary, to advance under the maximum possible protection of the maximum possible array of mechanical resources, in the form of guns, machine-guns, tanks, mortars and aeroplanes.'*
>
> General Sir John Monash, 1920

The level of human loss at the Battle of Fromelles is completely unacceptable in modern wars. Today, the death of a single Australian soldier in Iraq or Afghanistan is headline news. Governments and armies have been forced to value life more highly.

Nearly 100 years after the 'war to end all wars', the world's political leaders still resort to war as a solution for international disputes. Though soldiers are no longer treated like a disposable resource, modern military weapons can kill more efficiently, and in modern wars it is civilian lives that are undervalued.

Soldiers are honoured, war is glorified, and new generations of soldiers step forward, willing to fight — willing to die.

:tle of Fromelles Site Today

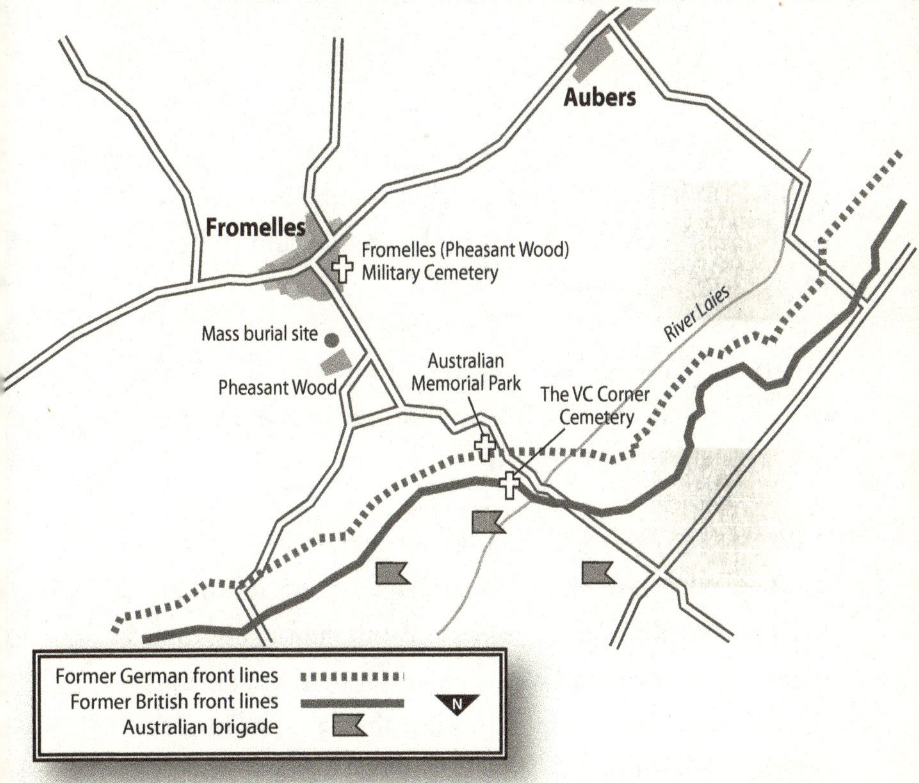

GLOSSARY

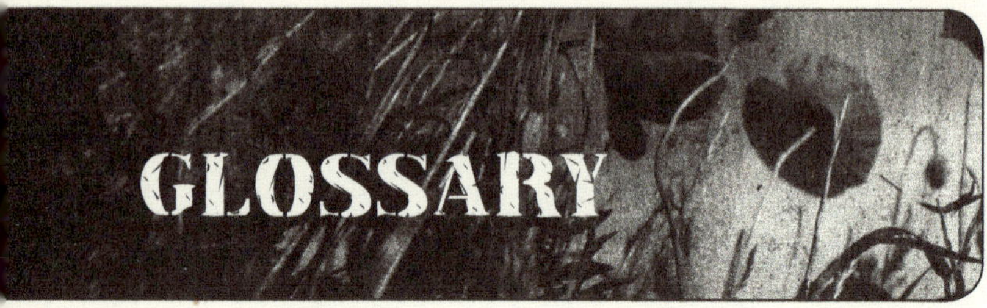

Allies, the All the countries that fought on the side of the French in World War I, including Britain, Belgium, Russia and Australia.

artillery Large guns that are mounted on a stand, wheels or a vehicle. Also the branch of the army that operates these guns.

AWOL Short for 'absent without leave'. This refers to soldiers who left their positions without permission. During World War I, soldiers from many countries, including Britain and New Zealand, could be sentenced to death by firing squad if they left their posts. Hundreds of Allied soldiers died like this. Australians, however, did not receive a death sentence for being AWOL.

barrage A heavy burst of artillery fire to protect one's advancing or retreating troops or to stop the advance of enemy troops.

battalion A unit of soldiers consisting of between 550 and 1,000 personnel.

battery A group of large guns operating together in a military operation.

billet Accommodation for a soldier in a private home or a non-military public building such as a school or town hall.

Blighty A slang word for England. In World War I, it also meant a small wound that was not life-threatening, but was serious enough for a soldier to be sent to a hospital in England.

bombs At the Battle of Fromelles this word refers to explosive devices thrown by hand or launched from mortars, i.e. grenades and mortar shells. The practice of dropping bombs from aircraft was still being developed in early World War I.

bombardment To attack with artillery fire or bombs.

brigade A unit of soldiers consisting of between 2,500 and 5,000 personnel.

bully beef Tinned corned beef.

canteen A small container for carrying water. In World War I, a soldier's canteen was made of aluminium.

cartridge A projectile fired from a hand gun which consists of a metal casing containing explosive material and a bullet. When the gun is fired the explosive propels the bullet, leaving the casing behind to be ejected.

company A unit of soldiers consisting of between 100 and 125 personnel.

concussion Jarring of the brain as a result of a blow or a fall. Also, any violent shaking or hard blow.

corps [pronounced 'cor'] A unit of soldiers consisting of two or more divisions.

court martial A military court where officers try soldiers convicted of breaking military laws.

division A unit of soldiers consisting of between 10,000 and 20,000 personnel.

dixie Another name for a mess tin. A portable metal saucepan, usually rectangular, which soldiers use for cooking or boiling water when on military operations.

enfilade Gunfire which is directed from the flank of

a battlefield along a length of trench or other formation of soldiers.

feint A fake action in a military operation to distract or mislead the enemy.

fire step A narrow step cut into the side of a trench for soldiers to stand on in order to lift themselves up so they can fire over the parapet.

flank The side or edge of a military formation, which is often vulnerable to attack because weapons are aimed forward.

garrison To position soldiers in a place such as a trench, a fort or a town in order to defend it.

infantry Soldiers who fight on foot with small weapons such as rifles and grenades.

latrine A toilet in a military camp or barracks.

militia Citizens trained for military service, but not members of the army, intended to be used in military emergencies.

offensive A military action against the enemy.

out-flank To go around the edge of an enemy position

in order to attack them from the side or from the rear.

parapet A defensive wall or fortification.

provost A military policeman.

referendum (plural: referenda) When a government seeks the opinion of the people by putting a question to the vote.

shell A hollow, cylindrical metal casing filled with explosive material or shrapnel to be shot from a large gun and designed to explode in flight or on impact.

shell shock Psychological strain caused by a traumatic experience, such as participation in warfare.

shrapnel Small bullets or spherical pieces of metal contained in a shell.

traverse A double turn in a trench to create protection for soldiers from side-on attack or to lessen the impact of an explosive device.

zero hour The time set for the beginning of a military attack, especially when more than one unit will be operating together.

Bibliography

Bean, C E W, 1941, *Official History of Australia in the War 1914–1918, Vol. III*, 'The Australian Imperial Force in France, 1916', 12th edition, at Australian War Memorial website, http://www.awm.gov.au/histories/first_world_war/volume.asp?levelID=67889

Bean, C E W, 1981 reprint, *Anzac to Amiens*, at Australian War Memorial website, http://www.awm.gov.au/histories/first_world_war/volume.asp?levelID=67901

Beaumont, Joan (ed.), 1995, *Australia's War, 1914–18*, Allen & Unwin, St Leonards, NSW

Bridger, Geoff, 2009, *The Great War Handbook: A Guide for Family Historians and Students of the Conflict*, Pen & Sword, Barnsley, South Yorkshire

Bull, Stephen, 2003, *World War I Trench Warfare 1914–1916*, Osprey, London

Butler, A G, 1940, *Official History of the Australian Army Medical Services, 1914–1918, Vol. II*, 'The Western Front' at Australian War Memorial website, http://www.awm.gov.au/histories/first_world_war/volume.asp?levelID=67899

Carlyon, Les, 2006, *The Great War*, Pan Macmillan Australia, Sydney

Chambers, Stephen J 2005, *Uniforms and Equipment of the Imperial German Army in World War I; A Study in Period Photographs*, Schiffer, Atglen PA

Cobb, Paul, 2007, *Fromelles 1916*, Tempus, Stroud, Gloucestershire

Corfield, Robin S, 2009, *Don't Forget Me, Cobber: The Battle of Fromelles*, Miegunyah Press, Melbourne

Downing, W H, c.1920, *To the Last Ridge*, Champion, Melbourne

Edmonds, Sir James E & Miles, Wilfred, 1932–38, *History of the Great War Based on Official Documents by Direction of the Historical Section of the Committee of Imperial Defence: Military Operations France and Belgium 1916*, Macmillan, London

Elliott, Major-General H E, 'The Battle of Fleurbaix' in *The Duckboard*, September, 1930

Ellis, A D, 1919, *The Story of the Fifth Australian Division: Being an Authoritative Account of the Division's Doings in Egypt, France and Belgium*, Hodder and Stoughton, London http://www.archive.org/details/storyoffifthaust00ellirich

Gammage, Bill, 1975, *The Broken Years: Australian Soldiers in the Great War*, Penguin, Melbourne

Kidd, Neville, 2000, *An Impression That Will Never Fade:*

The True Story of an Original Anzac, Neville Kidd, Pymble, NSW

Knyvett, R Hugh, 1918, *'Over There' with the Australians*, Hodder and Stoughton, London

Lee, Roger, 2010, *The Battle of Fromelles 1916*, Australian Army Campaign Series 8, Army History Unit, Canberra

Lindsay, Patrick, 2008, *Fromelles*, Hardie Grant, Melbourne

McMullin, Ross, 2002, *Pompey Elliott*, Scribe Publications, Carlton Nth, Vic.

Monash, General Sir John, 2009, *The Australian Victories in France 1918*, Naval and Military Press, East Sussex

Pederson, Peter, 2004, *Fromelles*, L Cooper, Barnsley, South Yorkshire

Pegler, Martin, 1996, *British Tommy 1914–18*, Osprey, London

Travers, Richard, 2001, *Diggers in France: Australian Soldiers on the Western Front*, ABC Books, Sydney

Wartime, Issue 44, 2008, various articles, Australian War Memorial

Wilkinson, Frederick, 1978, *A Source Book of World War I Weapons and Uniforms*, Wardlock, London

Williams, J F, 'Words on "a lively skirmish": Fromelles in Contemporary and Foreign Reports' in *Journal of the*

Australian War Memorial, 23 Oct 1993

Woolley, Charles, 1999, *Uniforms and Equipment of the Imperial German Army in World War I 1900–1918: A Study in Period Photographs*, Schiffer, Atglen PA

Wray, Christopher, 2002, *Sir James Whiteside McCay: A Turbulent Life*, Oxford University Press, Melbourne

Websites

Australian Army http://www.army.gov.au/fromelles

Firstworldwar.com: A Multimedia History of World War I http://www.firstworldwar.com

Fromelles Fallen, ABC, http://www.abc.net.au/news/events/fromelles

Lest We Forget: Virtual Fromelles Museum http://www.lestweforget.com.au

Oxford Archaeology http://thehumanjourney.net/index.php?option=com_content&task=view&id=536&Itemid=40

Remembering Fromelles, Commonwealth War Graves http://www.cwgc.org/fromelles/?page=english/homepage

The Long, Long Trail: The British Army of 1914–1918 for Family Historians http://www.1914-1918.net

World War I 1914–1918, Australian War Memorial http://www.awm.gov.au/atwar/ww1.asp

INDEX

Quote Citations

p.10 *The Argus*, 15 December 1915, p.9
p.13 *The Brisbane Courier*, 22 December 1915, p.6
p.20 quoted in Bean, 1941, vol. III, chpt. II, p.33
p.20 from the diary of Major Roy Harrison, quoted in Kidd, p,209
p.27 Knyvett, p.140
p.29 quoted in Bean, 1941, vol. III, chpt. XII, p.328
p.32 Knyvett, p.152
p.39 quoted in Bean, 1941, vol. III, chpt. XII, p.339
p.40 Bean 1941, vol. III, chpt. XII, p.336
p.51 Downing, p.24
p.52 Downing, p.18
p.58 quoted in Corfield, p.177
p.67 1. Quoted in Gammage p. 157
2. *Sydney Morning Herald*, 26 July 1919, p.7
p.71 quoted in McMullin, p.216
p.72 Downing, p.18
p.73 quoted in Corfield, p.240
p.75 quoted in Carlyon, p.82
p.83 Ellis, p.101
p.84 Knyvett, p.157
p.85 Downing, p.30
p.91 quoted in Carlyon, p.85
p.92 quoted in Corfield, p.194
p.98 Bean 1941, vol. III, chpt. XIII, p.438
p.101 quoted in Butler, p.46
p.104 quoted in Bean, 1941, vol. III, chpt. XIII, p.395
p.106 quoted in Ellis, p.81
p.107 quoted in Ellis, p.81
p.108 1. Quoted in Cobb, p.162
2. Elliott, p. 13
p.111 quoted in Carlyon, p.62
p.118 Letter to Bean, quoted in Carlyon, p.97
p.119 quoted in Carlyon, p.98
p.123 quoted in Lindsay, p.157
p.124 quoted in Bean, 1941, vol. III, chpt. XIII, p.444
p.125 quoted in Cobb, p.161
p.134 quoted in Corfield, p.210
p.135 quoted in Corfield, p.56
p.136 quoted in Lindsay, p.49
p.138 quoted in Corfield p.194
p.139 Edmonds p.134
p.142 Downing, p.22
p.152 quoted in *Wartime*, issue 44, 2008, p.17
p.155 quoted in Lindsay, p.474
p.160 quoted in Lindsay, p.442
p.161 Monash, p.96

Image Credits

Cover: Poppies / Shutterstock; p.iv: Private Brear, AWM; p.11: Troops bound for war, Hulton-Deutsch Collection / Corbis; p.15: *The Trumpet Calls*, Wikimedia Commons; p.18: *The Argus*, National Library of Australia; p.27: French woman serving coffee, AWM; p.30: German recruitment poster, Library of Congress; p.33: Unidentified soldier in trench, AWM; p.34: Soldiers moving field gun, Corbis; p.47: SMLE rifle, AWM; p.49: MG 08 machine gun, AWM; p.53: Trench mortar class, AWM; p.55: British recruitment poster, unidentified source; p.68: The 53rd Battalion, AWM; p.88: Fromelles battlefield, AWM; p.89: Next-of-kin plaque, AWM; p.102: *Opfertag* poster, Corbis; p.109: CEW Bean, AWM, p.127: Pigeon loft, AWM; p.137: Hitler in WWI, Wikimedia Commons; p.141: French poster, unidentified source; p.143: Soldiers with French children, AWM; p.155: Boot with sock, aapimages; p.159: Cobbers statue, aapimages; p.180: Carole Wilkinson, John Wilkinson

carole WILKINSON

Carole Wilkinson is an award-winning author of books for children. She has a long-standing interest in the history of everything. Carole was a laboratory assistant in a previous life, and is a meticulous researcher who finds it difficult to stop researching and begin writing.

Carole's best-selling 'Dragonkeeper' series has been translated into eleven different languages and has been published in over fifteen countries. *Dragonkeeper* and *Dragon Moon* were both winners of the Children's Book Council Book of the Year award for younger readers.

Carole is the author of several non-fiction titles on subjects as diverse as Ned Kelly, Alexander the Great and the modern Olympics. Carole's edited version of *Ned Kelly's Jerilderie Letter* was shortlisted for the Eve Pownall Award for Information Books. She has also written The 'Ramose' series, a fictional series set in Ancient Egypt.

Carole lives in Melbourne with her husband John and dog Rita, and is an ambassador for the Victorian Premier's Reading Challenge.

Carole Wilkinson and the *Cobbers* statue, Melbourne Shrine of Remembrance.

A Note from the Author

I am, as always, very grateful to all the historians whose thoughtful writing and thorough research made it possible for me to write this book. In particular, I would like to acknowledge the work of Australia's official World War I historian Charles Bean. His remarkable history of Australia's part in the war was an invaluable resource.

Thanks also to my editor Melissa Keil for her attention to detail and ever-present smile, and to Andrew Kelly for his support and encouragement. Thanks also to Neville Kidd and Damian Madden for their facts checking, Leigh MacCann of Hyland's military bookshop, and my good friend Dianne, who by a quirk of fate had an interest in World War I at the same time as I did, and was always willing to listen to me recounting my triumphs and frustrations.

Another important resource is the National Australian Archives (NAA) website which makes available the digitised records of all Australians who served in World War I. It is a wonderful service available for no charge.

If you would like to search for the records of a relative or historical figure, go to the NAA Record Search webpage at:

http://www.naa.gov.au/collection/recordsearch/index.aspx

Click on the Search Now button.

Enter the person's name — surname, first name and middle names if known.

Enter 1914 to 1918 in the date boxes.

Click on Search.

Scroll down the results list until you find the right person.

Click on the page icon in the column headed Digitised Image. This will open up a digital copy of the person's army record.

Click on the arrow button at the top or the bottom of the page to advance through the pages.

The characters of Private McAlister and Sergeant Crawford in the stories at the beginning of each chapter are fictitious. Their experiences are based on an amalgam of soldiers' experiences. The wording of the condolence letter written by Sergeant Crawford is based on the letter sent to my great grandmother when her son (my great uncle John) was killed in France towards the end of the war.